To Wendy and Joyce, the lessons began with you.

To Neal and Jamie, you are the best!

To Kerry, through tsunami, earthquake, flood, and pestilence, you have always been next to me. What an adventure!

CONTENTS

ACKNOWLEDGMENTS

I am humbled by the small army that aided me in producing this book: Sharon Morgenthaler started me on this adventure. David Horbovetz saw the book in me. Rita Emmett showed me the way. Maureen Cunningham would not let me quit. Rachel Krausman and Christopher Polinski helped me capture my stories. Jenna Glatzer, book saver, provided the editing.

Lynn Johnston, the best literary agent ever, showed patience and forbearance as she turned a soldier into an author.

Casey Ebro and the team at McGraw-Hill, thank you for the courage in publishing the book.

My undying gratitude to the great Soldiers, Sailors, Marines, Airmen, and Coastguardsmen that I have served with over the years and across continents.

Introduction

My Story

There aren't many kids who get to say that one of their parents is a spy. It's the stuff of television shows and movies and games kids play with each other. But for my father, it was a career. He was an infantry officer who conducted military intelligence operations for the United States Marines at the Pentagon. I thought his job was the coolest thing ever.

He would disappear on secret missions that he never told the family about. Even my mother didn't know where her husband was going or what he was doing when he got there, and she was supposed to just deal with that kind of uncertainty until he showed up again. For her, I'm sure it was nerve-racking. Although I missed my father when he was gone, I didn't worry—I was too naive to realize the dangers involved, and young enough to have a very romanticized view of what spy work was all about.

I imagined him as one of the dashing heroes on my favorite TV shows and movies: *The Man from U.N.C.L.E.*, *The Wild Wild West*, *Get Smart*, and of course James Bond. More likely, my dad was doing research and analysis, but in my mind, he was calculating angles so a bullet would ricochet off a bottle and whiz right past a villain's ear, scaring him into spilling the secret code needed to defuse a bomb about to go off in a theater.

There were, of course, pluses and minuses for me with a Marine officer for a dad. The first minus was that he missed my birth because he was off fighting in the Korean War. Luckily, I don't remember that. What I do remember is that I had a sheltered life growing up on military bases. All our needs were covered, and we didn't socialize with nonmilitary kids.

Many military wives wore their husband's rank, and bases were well segregated—officers with officers, enlisted men with enlisted men. Our housing was separated according to this hierarchy, so I could only socialize with other kids whose fathers were around the same rank as my father's, and it translated to a certain snobbery. The wives of colonels looked down on the wives of majors, and so on. My parents weren't like that, though. I remember going to the beauty parlor after my father had been promoted to major, and the ladies in the shop asked me who my mother was.

"Joyce Harvey Morgenthaler," I told them.

"She's the nicest woman here!" one of the beauticians exclaimed. "She never treats us badly because our husbands are enlisted."

The other ladies nodded. I was very proud of my mother that day, and it taught me something about the kind of person I wanted to be—the kind who would make people want to speak enthusiastically about me behind my back.

I was never much of a girly girl growing up in the 1950s and 1960s. Luckily, both my parents were feminists and never expected me to conform to society's "rules" for girls. But as parents, their gender roles were pretty standard: He barked out the orders that she followed, and if I wanted emotional support, I'd better talk to my mom, because my dad wouldn't put up with any *feelings*. "Suck it up" was the general theme.

"Daughters of Marines don't cry!" he would tell me. Later, it became "Daughters of Marine *colonels* don't cry!"

And Dad was never wrong.

Except that one time.

I was about 14, and we were sitting at the dining room table for dinner, with the television in the background showing the rerun of a boxing match. Later, my dad mentioned the winner of the match—except he named the wrong guy.

"He didn't win," I said.

"Of course he did!"

"But . . . I just watched it on television. The other guy won."

"It's in the newspaper," he said gruffly. "Go to the living room and go get the paper and look it up and you'll see I'm right. GO LOOK."

I turned to the sports page, and I was terrified . . . because *I* was right. I knew how to deal with my father when I was wrong, but how was I supposed to break the news to him that he was about to lose his always-right streak?

"WELL?" he boomed from the dining room in his Marine voice. "WAS I RIGHT?"

"No," I said in the tiniest voice I could manage. "I was."

I looked down at my feet as I brought in the newspaper. He grabbed it. For a moment, his face was serious, and then he burst out laughing. From then on, we were allowed to say that Dad had been wrong only once in his life.

That's why it was confusing to me when he told teenage me, "You're going to go further in life than I ever did."

Dad was wrong only once, so . . . could it be true?

═══════

"They're opening up the ROTC to women on a trial basis," my father told me, his eyes lit up with possibility. The move to an all-volunteer force had led to aggressive recruitment strategies. The military needed more bodies, even if they were female.

I thought for a few seconds about what he was telling me. I had never before considered a career in the military.

"Every branch?" I asked him.

"Every branch except the Marines."

"Then I'm not interested."

I was the daughter of a Marine, and I'd been brought up to believe that the Marines were the best.

But sometime between that conversation in summer and the day I arrived as a freshman at Penn State in September 1972, I had a change of heart. I walked up to the Willard Building, which housed the ROTC programs. My choice was simple: I didn't like flying and I was prone to seasickness, so I chose the Army.

"I want to be a spy," I told the officer. I wanted to do the top secret stuff my father was doing at the Pentagon.

"You should apply for a scholarship," he said. "This year is the first year we're offering four-year scholarships to women."

I had to go before the board that would decide on the scholarship recipients. Several young women went for their interviews before I did, and they chatted about their experiences afterward.

"What did they ask you?"

"Well, they wanted to know if I'd ever seen *M*A*S*H* and what I thought of it, and they asked me what I think the military does."

Softball questions. No worries—I had this thing nailed. I wasn't even nervous until I sat down in front of a seemingly completely different board from the one all the other women had appeared before.

"Do you think you're superior to these other girls because your father's an officer?" one of the men asked me.

I was confused. Was it just my perception, or were they . . . hostile? "The advantage is that I've moved a lot and I'm able to adapt and assess situations, but the disadvantage is that I have no lifelong friends, and that's kind of lonely," I replied.

I never got the *M*A*S*H* question. They fired away at me for several minutes until I walked away wondering what had just happened. But I must have had the right answers, because I became one of the first group of six women to receive a four-year scholarship to Penn State.

My grandfather Wendell P.C. Morgenthaler Sr. was too old to serve in World War II. He was thrilled when my father was accepted in the U.S. Naval Academy and later commissioned as a Marine Corps officer. My grandfather became a recruiter for the Academy and a regular at the officers club in Harrisburg. When he learned that I had followed in Dad's footsteps, he called me to tell me how proud he was. He requested a press release and photo from the ROTC brigade that he could send to his local newspaper—his granddaughter, one of the first scholarship recipients! He invited me to visit and met me at the bus terminal with flowers. He couldn't wait to take me to the officer's club and show me off to all the guys. But what a shock it was for both of us to see the following day's newspaper.

When you want people to salute in the Army, you say, "Present arms!" Under the women's picture ran the caption "Present legs!"

I hated seeing my grandfather humiliated—and I was none too pleased about it either. Our Army scholarships were a significant leap toward equality for women, and the newspaper staff had seen fit to trivialize it by making silly sexual commentary.

I hoped that the men I would serve with would not make that same judgment, but my dad was not so sure. As thrilled as my parents were for me, he warned me: "They don't want you there."

"What do you mean?"

"Most of the men don't want to see women in the military. You're going to have to work harder than everyone else to get any respect."

Doubts crept in. Was I making the right decision? It wouldn't take long to be tested: Soon after I signed up, I learned that those of us on scholarship were expected to join an extracurricular activity: either the Rangers or the drill team. I happily signed up for the Rangers—I couldn't wait to play war in the woods, learn survival skills, and lead other cadets. Army Rangers are some of the toughest people in the military.

But the colonel who led the Army ROTC brigade informed me that this was not an option for women. I was to join the drill team, period. I had already learned in class that I was not particularly good at marching; I lost the cadence too easily. So I pressed the issue, stressing that I had grown up playing war and that I wanted to be prepared for battle.

"Women are not in combat," he told me. It was a rule. No women in battle, therefore no training for battle.

I didn't know then how false his information was. Now I know about the nurses under attack at Anzio in World War II, the WACs wounded in Vietnam, and the women serving along the North Korean border. I'm sure they'll be glad to know that they weren't in combat after all.

"If I can't be in the Rangers, then I'm not doing an extracurricular activity," I told the colonel.

He lost it.

"You spoiled Marine brat! You think you're special? Your father's a stupid jarhead, and he doesn't get you any special treatment here. *I'm* in charge here, and you will follow my orders!"

My words were low and deliberate. "I'm not going to be some cutie marching around for your pleasure. You can take back the scholarship."

"You are dismissed," he said through clenched teeth.

I headed to the bathroom and had a good cry. Then I calmed down, washed my face, and headed to the military class already in session. Afterward, the colonel asked the instructor how I appeared in class. The captain was puzzled and said I seemed fine. Word flew throughout the brigade that I had stood up to the colonel. I didn't sign up for the drill team, and I didn't lose my scholarship. It was my first military victory.

———

My career would be punctuated by moments just like that. Along with the other pioneering women who joined alongside me, I had to redefine women's roles and prove that we were good for more than just tending wounds and filing papers. When things were unfair, we had to stand up for ourselves loudly, or no one else would.

At Penn State, some of the male cadets nicknamed one woman cadet "Tits" and another "Hot Lips." When a cadet tried to nickname me "Legs," I told him he could call me anything he wanted after I knocked his teeth in. This happened about two years before any U.S. court recognized sexual harassment as a crime: before that, bosses were free to fire employees who wouldn't sleep with them, and managers could make lewd remarks to their workers all day long without fear of reprisal. This was particularly evident in the military, where we women were expected to sing along with the obscene call-and-response cadences for marching or running ("I don't know but I've been told . . ."). Some of the officers used just the funny, PG versions, but many made unabashed references to women's genitals, and we were expected to get with it or quit.

I learned to pick my battles.

I never said anything about the cadences or the inappropriate sexual talk around us, but I did speak up when someone crossed the line with me personally, including once when a major cornered me and once when an officer pulled the women aside and told us that if we passed out in the field, then he would cut off our shirts and bras. Uh, *no*. There was no medical reason for that.

It's not that I was supremely confident—I had moments of doubt just like anyone else might, but I was determined never to become a victim of that doubt. For any meaningful change to happen, we women would have to be strong leaders, or else we would always be treated as lesser soldiers.

In my first year, the higher-ups pulled women out of weapons training to listen to classroom lectures, including one about weather balloons. I remember it specifically because all of us women nodded off at one point in the class and the poor professor said, "You must not have had much sleep last night." He was right, but we were also really tired of taking time-filler classes when what we should have been doing was training for battle. None of us wanted to be unprepared. A war does not choose its victims by gender.

So we yelled about it, loud and long. The following year, women weren't pulled out of combat training classes anymore. Progress.

Getting taken seriously wasn't our only problem, though. On my first assignment in Korea in 1977, I encountered another major problem: prostitution. Married men were openly cheating on their wives (calling it "geographical bachelorhood"); single young men were handing over their whole paychecks at the brothels. They'd bring strippers and prostitutes into the clubs and had no concern about how that would make the rest of us women feel.

What it did was sour me on the idea of marriage: It seemed that all the men were cheating, so why bother with marriage? It also seemed that they'd lost the very notion of women as people. I had nearly every man in the officers' club competing for my affection. I'd never had that much attention in my life! But it wasn't because they all cared about me or even had any idea who I was. To them, I was just a warm body, and because I was an American, I was "free." Prostitutes cost money.

When I was a junior officer, the same men who fell all over themselves to sweet-talk me at night would try to avoid saluting me during the day.

In the military, you are always supposed to stop what you're doing and salute any officer who outranks you. Instead, the guys would pretend not to see me, or just say, "Afternoon, Ma'am," an intentional slight.

All of it left me depressed, and I handled it badly. I gained weight so men would leave me alone and stop thinking of me as a sexual object, and I began waiting in the building until everyone else had left so I wouldn't have to encounter the enlisted men on my way out and feel their disrespect.

But one day, I got tired of being depressed. I thought about the gift my father had sent me when I arrived in Korea: a notebook that said, "Make Policy, Not Coffee!" I thought about the many great leaders I admired and how none of them would shy away from conflict.

If you let those guys get away with it once, they win, I told myself. It was crazy that I was hiding out in a building because some men didn't want to show respect. So the next time it happened, I made sure to counter it quickly.

"Oh!" I said. "You've forgotten how to salute. Well, that's OK because I can show you. Come here, soldier."

I made him salute over and over and over again. This went on for an extraordinary length of time—and soon word spread among the enlisted men that you probably should just salute Lieutenant Morgenthaler or she'd waste your whole afternoon.

===

At every turn, I was well aware of the consequences of my performance. Whatever I did or failed to do had the potential to change the future for all the women who would come after me. If I showed emotion, my commanders would not say that Jill Morgenthaler showed emotion; they would say that *women* are too emotional.

I knew that my father had been right—I would have to work twice as hard for half the recognition. So instead of complaining about it, that's what I set out to do: I shot my hand in the air to volunteer for everything, took my work as seriously as I'd taken my studies, pushed past my comfort zone, and applied for promotions.

My life in the military was full of many "firsts": I was the first female company commander in the Army Security Agency Group Korea serving along the Korean Demilitarized Zone (DMZ), the first female battalion commander in the 88th Regional Support Command, and the first female brigade commander in the 84th

Division, commanding hundreds of soldiers across six states. In Illinois, I was the first woman to lead homeland security.

Between 1976 and my retirement in 2006, I served in command centers in Korea, Germany, Bosnia, and Iraq, earning the Legion of Merit and the Bronze Star. It was meaningful to me to know that my work was saving lives and bringing people freedom.

You might think that after all my years of service, sexism would be much less of a problem, but consider this: After the birth of my second child, I took off one weekend from the Reserve unit—*two days* when I was entitled to months of maternity leave. I came back to find that my position had been filled and I'd been demoted—under the patronizing guise of making my life "less stressful." Do they do that to men who become fathers? I didn't accept the demotion and instead transferred to a different department, where I continued working my way up according to plan.

Never did I accept the limitations that others tried to impose on me, whether in the military or in my civilian work. Along the way, I met a wonderful man who supports everything I do (though he does have to remind me every now and then to check my "commanding officer" persona at the door), had two great kids who are now successful young adults, attained the rank of full colonel in 2000, ran for Congress (I won the primary, though not the seat), and became a professional public speaker.

I've learned many lessons in the military about how to earn respect, rally a team, overcome opposition, and more, and I will share these with you. They have served me well in business life as well, because good leadership is good leadership. The same interpersonal skills, work ethic, and mindset apply, which is why I've been able to train others to be more effective managers and business owners.

I've seen a lot in this lifetime: rich and poor, just and unjust, oppressed and free, war and peace, the privileged and the marginalized. I've learned from each person I've met, and all of it has led me to the kind of life I'm proud to be living.

And I got to be a spy after all.

1

OVERCOMING OBSTACLES

The Army had just started letting women in, so I knew I'd be something of a rarity when I departed for officer boot camp in the summer of 1975, right after my junior year in college. But I didn't account for just *how* rare: There were 83 female cadets on a military base of 50,000 men, and as my father had warned me, many of the men were not prepared to sissify the Army with women. I was called every name in the book: bitch, butch, bimbo, and those were just the names beginning with the letter *b*.

Obstacles? Heck, yes. Showing my face on the first day was facing an obstacle. Boot camp is no picnic for anyone, but there was an extra dimension when I realized that some people didn't want to "break us down to build us back up," but rather just to break us down and get us to leave as quickly as possible. Not only was I determined to stay; I was set on learning what it took to be a great leader. What put me on track was my first military role model.

I was assigned to one of the few companies that had women: four women in a company of 36. I was in a squad with eight men.

The commander, a field artillery captain, was not sure what to do with the four women in his company, but I lucked out with his first sergeant. Sergeant Sampson took his job seriously: to train cadets to lead. He had risen through the ranks in the 1960s and received a field commission as an officer in the Vietnam War. Although he was reduced in rank after the war because there were too many junior officers, he continued to serve as a sergeant rather than retiring. He never told us this, but I know he suffered extreme prejudice growing up black in the 1940s and 1950s and serving in the 1960s and 1970s. He knew firsthand what it meant to be harassed, abused, and worse. Sergeant Sampson did not allow harassment of the female cadets; he worked to train every one of us to succeed. Woman or man, he kept his eye on each one of us, so no one was left behind.

Leaving no one behind is a key concept in the military, especially when you're talking about life-or-death situations, but it's also a hallmark of good leadership in business. Overlooking a team member who doesn't "get it," ignoring someone's input, letting any of your workers trash-talk or belittle any other workers, or playing favorites can severely demoralize your team and make junior members less likely to be invested in the company's success. A good leader strives to overlook no one and bring out the best in everyone.

DON'T EXPECT "EASY"

The six weeks of camp consisted of war games, weapons training, and obstacle courses; the latter especially were our proving ground. There were obstacle courses for individuals and for teams, and they were designed to test us physically and emotionally.

On my first day on the individual obstacle course, I jogged to the first obstacle called the Belly Robber. It looked deceptively easy. The Belly Robber was made of five rolling logs bolted horizontally to a frame three feet above the ground. To get across, I just had to roll my body along each log.

I lay prone, belly down on the first log, and used my stomach and arms to roll to the next log. The logs rotated easily—too easily. Whoops, I almost rolled under the second log. Wait a minute . . . this was hard! If I slipped under, I could get hurt. If I slipped off, I would have to start over.

As I reached for the next log, using my belly and thighs to steady me, I could hear my teammates encouraging me. I shut out their voices and focused. I narrowed my vision, looking only at the log immediately in front of me. Intense concentration synchronized my body with my mind. I grasped, slid, crawled, and made it to the next log, and then the next one. I turned it into a game of concentration: thought, action, repeat. One log conquered. Next log conquered. At the end, I dismounted feet first and hollered, "Hooah!"

"Hooah" is a term in the Army that when used as a statement means "I got it," "I understand," or "Will do." When used as a question, hooah translates into "Do you agree?" or "Do you understand?"

What I learned from the first obstacle was not to underestimate it and not to look too far ahead. It is important to stay focused on the task at hand.

This is true in wider applications: When you believe something is going to be easy, you can get complacent. Cocky. You don't put in as much attention or focus as you should, and you can wind up rolling under that log pretty easily. Every challenge deserves your attention until it is solved; there are many problems that will seem easy. Stay on the ball. Focus on what's in front of you, so that it's done right before you mentally skip right past it.

I jogged to the next obstacle, the Island Hopper. Again, the obstacle seemed simple, but this time I knew better. The Island Hopper consisted of stumps ranging from 6 to 26 inches above the ground, unevenly placed from the near side to the far side of the course. The mission was to complete the course by jumping from one stump to another without touching the ground.

I had played a similar game at home with my brother and sisters. We would jump from sofa to chair to coffee table, never touching the freshly vacuumed rug. Would this be as easy? I nimbly jumped on the first stump, jumped to the next one, and fell off. I had to start over. I jumped on the first stump and then the second and promptly fell off again. I went back to the beginning.

This time I waited at the start line. The corporal in charge came over and said, "Cadet, what's the problem?"

"I'm doing something wrong," I said.

"You're rushing it," he said. "Think before you leap."

I took his advice, jumped, got my balance, paused, jumped to the next stump, balanced, paused, and moved forward. I finished the obstacle easily. The key to finishing this obstacle was patience. The Island Hopper taught me not to assume that I knew the problem, but instead, to assess the situation, decide the plan of action, and then execute carefully.

FACING THE SCARY UNKNOWN

The next obstacle was called the Slide for Life. You know it now as zip-lining, a common tourist activity, but back in the 1970s, it was unknown except to the military. The zip line consisted of a thick wire suspended from a 40-foot-high tower, over a stream, down to the other side of the bank. A handlebar carried you swiftly down.

Standing in line, I started to inch behind the guys next to me. No way was I going first. A corporal saw me and yelled, "Blondie, you're first!" Later, I realized that I was often chosen first because if a woman did the challenge, then the men would follow without complaint. He shoved me to the front of the line, and I slowly climbed up the 40-foot tower. As I made my way to the edge of the platform, I felt nauseated.

The sergeant on the platform said, "Keep your legs parallel to the ground as you glide down. If you don't, you will break both legs when you hit the water. When you see the flag drop, let go and drop into the water. If you don't let go, then you will crash into the wire suspension system and smash your face. Understood?"

I squeaked out, "Hooah."

I think my eyes almost popped out of my head as he went through these instructions. I decided to be honest. "Sergeant, I'm scared. Can I opt out of this?"

"Yes, Cadet, you can."

I gasped with relief and disbelief. "Thank you, thank you, thank you, Sergeant."

The sergeant added, "Instead of doing this, Cadet, just give me a pull-up on the handlebar."

"Yes, sir!" I grabbed the bar, did a pull-up, and to my surprise, I went flying down the Slide for Life.

As I whizzed down, I remembered his gruesome instructions and lifted my legs parallel. When the white flag waved, I dropped into the stream. Thanks to the trickery of that sergeant, I had the ride of a lifetime. The sergeant would not let me opt out, and after I did it once, I was eager to go again. Unfortunately, I was told it was one ride per customer.

The unknown is the hardest obstacle of all. When we don't know what to expect, we lose the feeling of control. This is what really scares us the most—the loss of control. Kids are afraid of the dark because they don't know what might be hiding from sight. Similarly, when we don't know what to expect at the end of the rope, we feel the need to pull away from it. It is this fear of the unknown that stops our progress.

Over the course of the session, obstacles like Tough Nut, Dirty Name, Hip-Hip, and Skyscraper tested everything from balance to physical strength. But more than that, the obstacles were designed to test our mental stamina and perseverance. Were we cut out to be soldiers, or were we quitters? When under fire, would we wave the white flag or keep moving forward?

Several things give me the courage to do something when I'm afraid. I focus on the why, the reason I need to do the task. I remind myself that others have already accomplished the feat. If them, why not me? I take the fear and break it into manageable pieces. I stay focused on one step at a time. After completing the first step, I move to the next.

People have different temperaments, and you'll need more than a one-size-fits-all approach when helping someone on your team face a big challenge. For me, having my sergeant give me a little push and tricking me into doing the terrifying thing was the right move. He knew me well enough to realize that was the best approach—but it's not the right approach for everyone. Do that to some people and they'll freeze up in terror and never trust you again.

Get to know the people on your team individually, so you know what works best for them. Some need to talk things through and go over all the possible scenarios, others just need a good pep talk, while others need to see someone else do it first. Try different strategies to see what clicks.

———

Once everyone had completed the individual obstacles, I moved on to the team obstacles with my squad. The mission was to get every member of the squad from point A to point B by overcoming barriers. At each new training site, a different cadet was the leader and was graded on the success or failure of the team. When it was my turn to be the leader, I was excited about being in charge. But then, as we jogged up to point A, I stopped. Actually, I froze. The guys behind ran into me. As I looked at the obstacle, I was petrified. I was facing one of my worst fears—the fear of heights. A rope bridge swung over a 50-foot chasm. I don't know if the guys understood why I had stopped so suddenly, but Sergeant Samson did. He saw the panic in my eyes and knew I was in trouble. He walked over to me and, very quietly and very gently, whispered in my ear, "Are you a warrior or a wimp?" The question snapped me out of it. I yelled out, "Warrior! Hooah!"

Before I had a chance to dwell on my fear, I charged across the bridge. All the men followed me. The best moment was seeing the cadre waiting on solid ground ahead of me—especially officers who did not believe that women could lead—with their mouths literally hanging open at the sight of a woman charging toward them with men following. From Sergeant Sampson, I learned that the difference between a warrior and a wimp doesn't involve brawn. It involves your inner self. It begins with you. Wimps don't believe they can do it (whatever *it* is), while warriors keep trying.

The acronym OBSTACLE can help you overcome impediments:

O   Outline the nature of the roadblock.

B   Brainstorm solutions. Don't discount any ideas.

S   Select your advisors and experts to assist you in solving and implementing solutions.

T   Test the possibilities. Throw out the ones that are not doable.

A   Adopt the solution.

C   Communicate the solution with the team.

L   Leverage the success. Promote the team's achievements. Don't forget to celebrate.

E   Evaluate the outcome. Conduct a postmortem to determine what lessons were learned.

SOMETIMES YOU NEED THE LITTLE GUY

My team was considered handicapped because a woman (me) was on it. I was informed that I was the weakest link, but the guys on my squad were great. They never called me the names that others did. To them, I was the "little guy." I admit that I liked the title "little guy." The guys on my team were built like wedges: broad shoulders and narrow hips. I was just the opposite—a pyramid with little shoulders and curvy hips. At five-foot-seven and 145 pounds, I was flattered to be the "little guy." I knew in my heart that sometimes you need the little guy.

When we got to the next team obstacle, we stared at it with horror. We were standing in front of a wall of barbed wire, rip-your-clothes-and-flesh barbed wire. As if this were not enough, the ground beyond it was painted yellow to represent nuclear contamination. If you somehow got over, around, or under the barbed wire but touched the yellow, you were "dead" and the team failed. Our mission was to get the team over the barbed wire and across "contaminated land" to safety at point B. Suspended above the barbed wire was a rope. On the far safe side of the contaminated land was a plank of wood. The rope and plank were our only tools.

As a fan of *Star Trek*, I felt like we were in a Kobayashi Maru episode, a no-win scenario. On the television show (and later in the 2009 *Star Trek* movie), Captain James T. Kirk is the only cadet to conquer the no-win scenario because he slips into the space academy and rigs the machine. He cheats. With the barbed wire obstacle, I did not see a way across, and cheating was not an option. We all looked at each other in disbelief.

Fortunately, cadet Bob Mussorgsky, a Vietnam veteran who was transitioning from enlisted to officer and the biggest soldier in our squad, was the leader during that obstacle. He quickly assessed the situation and our strengths and told us his plan: "I'm the biggest guy. I'm going to throw myself on the barbed wire. Morgenthaler, you're the little guy. You're going to run up my back, swing across the contaminated area, drop down, grab the plank, and throw it back to us. Hooah?"

I said, "No hooah! Are you nuts? You're throwing your body on barbed wire? I'm running on you?"

"This is the only solution."

We all nodded assent. As Mussorgsky rolled down his sleeves and put his cap over his face, I started preparing to run as fast and as lightly as I could. I kept thinking of Muhammed Ali saying, "Float like a butterfly." Mussorgsky threw himself on the barbed wire. I ran up his back as fast as I could. I grabbed the rope and swung like Tarzan across the "contaminated" area, dropped down, grabbed the plank, and, with my adrenaline pumping, threw it up and across to him. He grabbed it, jumped off the barbed wire, and lay the plank on the wire, and the team ran across it. We all made it across easily within the time limit. We chest-bumped in celebration. (I learned how to chest-bump that day.) We had conquered barbed wire.

Then the officer in charge of the obstacle called the team together and told us that we had broken the camp record. The team with the little guy, the team with the handicap, the team with the *girl* had broken the record.

It's important to identify each of your team members' strengths. We are not all cut out to be the biggest and toughest, but if you look deeper, you are likely to find that everyone on your team has something useful to offer. If you're not sure, you might try *asking*. Speak with your team and ask, "What do you consider your best strengths?" or "What do you think you'd be really good at that you haven't gotten to do here yet?" The answers may be enlightening.

NO EXCUSES

When I reported to the experimental coed Army boot camp, I encountered a culture of rules and orders. It was the 1970s, and there was no questioning of authority. When a drill sergeant hollered, "When I say jump, you say how high," it meant that we

brothers had accepted throughout their lives. So when faced with controversy, Susan chose to defer to the school's choice.

I pointed out that the top graduate often receives better assignments. Another woman said that this wasn't about Susan but about how women should be treated and their accomplishments acknowledged. I stressed that this was an issue bigger than her receiving an award. If a woman is at the top of the class, it should

HOW WE VIEW ASSERTIVENESS ACROSS THE SEXES

This is a real concern and problem that remains as true today as it was in the 1970s. There is a gender discrepancy in how we see leaders and how we judge those who fight for what is owed to them. Men are "assertive"; women are "pushy." It was not fair then, and it is not fair now.

In a large-scale study, researchers from the Stanford Graduate School of Business revealed that the most successful women in business had to employ a double strategy: They exhibited characteristics that are stereotypically male, such as self-confidence and dominance, but had to show those traits only *sometimes*. They had to temper that with feminine behaviors as well, when the social situation called for it. The researchers called it "self-monitoring" and revealed that "masculine" women who were good at self-monitoring—the chameleons of the group—received 1.5 times the promotions of masculine men and 3 times the promotions of masculine women who were not good "self-monitors."

be recognized, not hidden away like a dirty secret. With those persuasive arguments, Susan was almost ready to speak to the commandant. Her next concern was for the lieutenant who had already been told he was the top student—she didn't want to upset him. I left to find him and speak with him, and to his credit, he did not want to receive an award he did not deserve. Her final concern was that the commandant would see her as "pushy" or "whiny."

I told Susan that several of us would go with her to see the commandant. We would make sure that the commandant understood that this was not about her per se but about fairness. I was sure that he would right the wrong—but that was wishful thinking. The system had been rigged so a woman could not be at the top of the class. When the four of us explained the mistake to the commandant and asked him to rectify it, he said no and downplayed the importance of the accomplishment.

"Besides," he said, "there isn't time to change the plaque or the graduation program."

Each one of us spoke up, making an argument about why the mistake was unethical and unacceptable. The commandant told us not to get our "panties in a twist" and dismissed us. Having grown up in the military, I knew that there was one more place we could turn for resolution. I smiled and asked the commandant where the office of the Inspector General (IG) was. In the military, the IG oversees complaints of unethical behavior. The commandant thought about it and said that it wasn't necessary to involve the IG. He would make the change on the personnel records, but he would not change the graduation programs.

Incidentally, Susan went on to become a colonel.

In many fields, the system is still rigged against women. Unfortunately, many women are afraid to challenge the system.

They were raised to sit quietly and not make waves. In elementary school, they were taught that their voices weren't important. In 1993, American University professors Myra Sadker and David Sadker published their research in *Failing in Fairness: How America's Schools Cheat Girls*, showing that schools ingrained in girls that their answers were less valid than boys' answers. They reported, "Boys called out eight times as often as girls did. When a boy yelled out, the teacher ignored the 'raise your hand' rule and usually praised his contribution. Girls who called out got reminders to raise their hands. Teachers valued boys' comments more than girls' comments. Teachers responded to girls with a simple nod or an OK, but they praised, corrected, helped, and criticized boys."[1]

Moreover, women seek to get along. We want everyone to play nice. However, this backfires when injustice occurs to one woman and others are not willing to support her. When a woman has the chutzpah to stand up to right a wrong, she is called difficult or a pain in the rear. Her grievance or accomplishments are minimized.

One of the most important things leaders can do for women or anyone else in an "underdog" position is to provide backup at times like this. Sexism will not end if only half the population is speaking against it. Don't allow others to minimize the concerns of, name-call, or stereotype women. Speak up when you witness sexism, racism, ageism, or any other "ism." It can be very difficult to do, especially when you're speaking up to one of your superiors, but it's the only way change happens. Otherwise, it allows an unjust environment to flourish, which is poisonous to morale. Try speaking to the person about the remarks and give specific examples of when his or her language was inappropriate or crossed the line. If others will join you, the conversation will have greater impact.

One way to speak so people will listen is to approach the matter as if you believe the person has good intentions and is simply unaware of how something has come across. For example, you could say, "Mike, I know you're a respectful person, so I'm sure you didn't mean it when you made those comments about Jesse. But I believe you should rethink the way you've handled this, because it seems that you're refusing to promote him based on his sexual orientation and not on his qualifications, and that's against our policy. He's a strong worker, and he's earned that promotion."

More often than not, even when people are uncomfortable with sexist, homophobic, or racist "jokes" and comments, they kind of smile and go along with it because they don't want to be targeted next; but this kind of inaction becomes part of the problem. Even "jokes" need to be corrected. There's no room for discrimination in the workplace, even if it's seemingly done in jest.

WOMEN AGAINST WOMEN

Sometimes other women are our biggest detractors because they are afraid of the competition. I arrived at Fort Huachuca with 19 other women. Four others, including Susan, were ROTC graduates. Like me, they had spent four years learning to lead men and women. We had attended integrated Army officer boot camp and had overcome similar obstacles. The other 15 women were WACs. They had been together for a few months at Fort McClellan, Alabama, participating in segregated Women's Army Corps training. These women had neither trained with nor led men. The five of us from ROTC were confident junior officers. I could not say the same for some of the WACs; in fact, they were afraid they would fail.

One WAC, doubtful of her experience, lashed out at the five of us. She spent time during intelligence training sniping whenever one of us made a contribution in class. I came to realize that, besides being insecure, she was a "queen bee"—a woman who would not help other women because she believed only one woman could be at the top. The term "queen bee syndrome" was popularized two years before I attended military intelligence school. University of Michigan researchers coined the phrase as they studied the phenomenon of women working in male hierarchies preventing other women from rising to the top. This would not be the only example in the military that I experienced of women undermining women.

The five of us ignored her nasty remarks and focused on learning. However, she continued to put us down. One afternoon, I was under a jeep showing the class how to inspect it properly when I heard her make another snide remark. Although I desperately wanted to jump up and verbally rip into her, I knew that I would be the one who looked bad. Instead, after class, I went up to her privately and asked why she felt the need to put me down. I told her my goal was to cooperate and graduate. I appealed to her professionalism and asked what I could do so we could get along. She was surprised to be called on her actions, and she stopped the behavior.

If your boss is a queen bee, and she is showing preference for the male employees, confronting her will take finesse. Make an appointment. Calmly state that you feel she has a double standard. If she becomes defensive, ask her what you can do to improve your performance. Avoid being confrontational at all costs. Accept any feedback you receive graciously. She may not have realized what she was doing; sometimes it will take a little time to sink in, but she may think it through later, figure out you were right, and correct her behavior.

USING REASON INSTEAD OF ANGER

I reached out to the other WACs to help them catch up. We soon bonded over a common enemy: Captain "Grizzly" was a hard-charging Special Forces officer who had volunteered and served three tours in Vietnam. He had moved up through the ranks from private and received a battlefield commission to lieutenant in Vietnam. He was a true hero—and a Neanderthal. In his forties, he was of the old school that held that the military was no place for a woman. Any woman who chose to serve was a lesbian or a slut or was mentally incapacitated.

At the end of class one day, Captain "Grizzly" told the women we had to stay after class. The men were released. We were puzzled. Captain "Grizzly" called us to attention and explained that we would be training in the desert shortly. He shocked us when he said, "If any of you broads collapse from heat exhaustion, I will use my knife and cut off your Army blouse, your T-shirt, and your bra."

What?

My immediate thought was, "You pervert. You just want an excuse to cut off our bras." We were stunned. He dismissed us and walked out. One of the older WACs had been a nurse before joining the military. She recovered first and said, "Let's all go to the commandant's office; this is outrageous."

We carpooled across post, and the 20 of us demanded to see the commandant immediately. He brought us in, and the former nurse calmly explained what had transpired and informed him that cutting our clothes off with a knife was not acceptable medical practice. As I watched her, I realized that the calm, intellectually based argument was a better approach than an angry mob demanding that the pervert be fired. I could see that the commandant was embarrassed, and he told us he would rectify it immediately. Captain "Grizzly" was transferred back to Special Forces, where he did not have to instruct women.

As a leader, you may find the system rigged against you or a member of your team. Voicing the unfairness is the first step. Respectfully and candidly letting the people in power know what is wrong and asking that it be corrected demonstrates self-confidence and dignity. This helps make others sensitive to the legitimacy of your outlook. It takes courage to be the dissenting voice, but that is how change for the good occurs. When no one speaks up and unfairness goes unchecked, it only gets worse. If possible, bring others with you who believe in fixing the wrong. Multiple voices give credence to the problem.

When you are having the difficult conversation, stay focused on the issue, remain calm, and rein in the emotions. You will be more successful if you keep the conversation focused on what is needed instead of who is to blame. Come prepared with ideas for solutions and as much evidence and backup for your position as possible. It's best to wait and gather your facts instead of rushing headlong into a confrontation based on anger or frustration.

Men, when you hear sexist remarks made to and about women, tell the offender to quit. Women, do the same when a woman makes an inappropriate remark about a man. Everyone should voice strong disapproval of racism and ethnically disparaging remarks. Leadership is about inclusion and respect.

3

Faking It

Most Americans do not know that we almost went to war again against the North Koreans from 1977 to 1978. Kim Jong-il was North Korea's leader. Not only had he threatened to nuke the United States several times, but the North Koreans had recently shot down one of our helicopters. Tragically, they ambushed and killed a U.S. lieutenant in the demilitarized zone (DMZ) between North Korea and South Korea.

My first assignment after military intelligence school was as a second lieutenant in South Korea in 1977. I flew into Seoul, where I was housed overnight. The next day, wearing my Class A uniform (green jacket with skirt—women's Class As did not come with slacks at that time), I went to an airfield where a helicopter was awaiting me. Trying to climb on the Huey in my skirt was a challenge to my modesty. As I strapped in, one warrant officer handed another a dollar bill. I'm sure my puzzled expression spoke for itself.

He said, "I bet the guys your underwear was blue, and I won." I felt degraded, but I planted a smile on my face. *Ha ha. Real funny, guys.* Later, after the guys in the unit became my friends, they gave me a men's flight uniform to wear as I flew around the country.

Camp Humphries housed the 501st Military Intelligence Brigade, which across South Korea conducted multidiscipline intelligence and security operations in support of the Eighth United States Army, U.S. Forces Korea, U.S. Army Pacific, and U.S. Pacific Command. I looked forward to being part of a very sophisticated intelligence gathering post that monitored the North Korean communist threat.

The commander of the brigade, Colonel Charles Black, was known throughout the military intelligence community as the "Prince of Darkness." I was assigned to work directly for him as his scheduler. He commanded units throughout South Korea, and I was responsible for the logistics of his travel, the arrangements for visiting VIPs, and briefing him daily on his appointments.

Colonel Black seemed to thrive on ripping into people of all ranks and positions. He would show up at units unannounced and give them holy hell if they weren't ready to brief him. I soon made it part of my job to warn subordinate units when he was heading to their sites, which earned me their trust. I think Colonel Black caught on. He started to slip out the back door without telling me. I would receive a call from a commander asking why I hadn't alerted them, which confused me—wasn't he right here? I would check his office and see that he had snuck out.

One morning, I received a call from the Pentagon telling me that the "Dixie" (that's what I heard) was flying into the Korean theater and would review what the command was doing. I did not ask who or what a Dixie was, but I put the appointment on the calendar

He stepped into my room and told me straight out, "Jilly Bear, they don't want you."

"Of course they want me," I said. "I've got my tickets; I've got my orders."

"No, sweetie. They do not want you. They are going to try and break you down. A lot of men think that if the military lets women in to lead men, then we will have a sissified military. If we have a sissy military, then the communists will easily defeat America."

"What do I do?"

"Why are you doing this?"

"To save lives and bring freedom. You know, like you."

"Don't forget that," he said.

"What do I do if I don't know what to do?"

"Look, you have talents. You're also the daughter of a Marine. When you don't know what to do, learn from the sergeants. Worst case, just fake it till you make it," he said.

Fortunately, my dad's advice was sound. I reminded myself that, first of all, I did OK at training. It was camp, not combat, but I did reasonably well. Then thinking about it some more, I remembered being in combat—sort of. As the daughter of a Marine, I grew up playing war in the red hills of Virginia. OK, it was not real, but I had gone through the motions with determination and confidence, and sometimes that's all you have to draw upon. I thought about being captain of the safety patrol in sixth grade. Sure, I was grasping at straws, but a little confidence was what I needed.

I walked into that office, sat down, and looked at the men— men who had never worked for a woman—and said with feigned confidence, "Gentlemen, let's save lives and bring freedom."

None of them snickered. All they saw was my (fake) bravado.

"Hooah," they said in unison.

FAKE IT TILL YOU MAKE IT

Today in corporate America, according to Jack Zenger writing in *Harvard Business Review*, the average age of someone made a leader is 30 years old, but the average age of someone receiving formal leadership training is 42 years old.

"But the average age of supervisors in these firms was 33. In fact, the typical individual in these companies became a supervisor around age 30 and remained in that role for nine years—that is, until age 39. It follows then, that if they're not entering leadership training programs until they're 42, they are getting no leadership training at all as supervisors. And they're operating within the company untrained, on average, for over a decade."[1]

So basically, *everyone* is faking it, at least in the beginning. What happens during the 12-year gap for those with leadership responsibility but no leadership training? What if today you are a hardworking team member, and tomorrow you are anointed a leader? How do you fill that training gap?

1. Provide the vision. You matter. Your leadership matters, and so does your ability to communicate to your team what matters. If you can show people why you are doing what you are doing and where you are going, they are more than likely going to follow you. As the leader, you provide the vision. Make it a vision that counts. I lucked out because my dad had provided me with a vision, and it was a clear, precise statement: save lives and bring freedom.

Your vision should be bigger than you. Ask yourself, "What do I want to contribute to others?" That is what makes it matter. It should be inspirational and something that people will take to heart. You probably already know that, but here is some advice you might not have considered: Your statement of what matters should be short and simple. That makes it easier to remember. Whenever you feel unsure, remind yourself and your team of what matters. Focus on that.

2. Remember you're in it together. Whenever you feel discouraged, remember it is not about you! You are responsible for a team, and you are in it together.

Commanders and coaches have a lot in common. Great coaches do four things well:

- They push the team players, having them go beyond their perceived limits.

- They pull the team players, giving a helping hand when needed.

- They encourage. Look at the word *encourage* again. Leaders put the courage in the team.

- Finally, they celebrate with praise, awards, and rewards.

3. Know your knacks. We all have gifts, talents, and experience. Do a leadership assessment to find out your leadership strengths. Additionally, examine your life and see where else you have led: school, sports, church, volunteer organizations.

So, what do *you* bring to the table? You might have to go far back like I did to become aware of your skills and talents. There are wonderful tools available online to find out what your talents are. When you are feeling insecure, remind yourself of your strengths. Think of how to put them to use.

4. Study your role models. What leaders have you worked for that you admire, and how can you emulate them? As a young offi-

LEARNING ABOUT YOUR STRENGTHS

Here are four websites you can visit to assess your strengths as a leader.

Strengths Based Leadership Assessment

www.strengthstest.com/strengthsfinderthemes/leadership-themes.html

Leadership Legacy Assessment

www.yourleadershiplegacy.com/assessment.html

How Good Are Your Leadership Skills? quiz

www.mindtools.com/pages/article/newLDR_50.htm

Leadership Self-Assessment Activity

www.nwlink.com/~donclark/leader/survlead.html

cer, I chose my father, Sergeant Sampson, and Captain Armstrong to emulate. I admired the teachings of Abraham Lincoln, who faced worse obstacles than I ever had. I try every day to live his words, "I do the very best I know how, the very best I can, and I mean to keep on doing so until the end."

I recommend that you study other successful leaders in your field. I researched General George Patton because his men would follow him into hell and back. His leadership style stressed that success is an attitude. "We will win because we never lose! There can never be defeat if a man refuses to accept defeat. Wars are lost in the mind before they are lost on the ground."

5. Visualize yourself as a leader. If you don't buy it, who else will? Start thinking of yourself as a competent, well-liked leader who understands how to get the best out of everyone on your team. Even if you don't feel this way deep down yet, act as if you do. It's been shown that acting confident helps you be confident. Act like a confident, proven leader because you will be one. Ask yourself what your favorite leader would do in the same situation.

WHEN YOU CAN'T SOLVE IT ALL

There are situations that one person can't solve. In 1977, the Army was rampant with racism and sexism. It seemed that overnight the Army realized there was this new thing called equal opportunity. The Army needed to train all soldiers to treat women and minorities the same as white men. The four-star general at Eighth Army ordered a conference on equal opportunity. Every command had to provide a representative to Seoul. My commander looked around, saw the only woman, and sent me.

I walked into a large conference room, and every person around the table and against the walls was an African American NCO. I was the only white person, only woman, and only officer in the room. Of course, the chair at the head of the huge conference table was the only seat left. I sat down and looked at all the black sergeants, they looked back, and I think we were all thinking, "OK, what now?" Then, a white male major rushed into the room and said, "We have racism in the Army here in Korea. You have three hours to come up with a solution. I expect a written report."

I watched in amazement as he left the room. All heads turned to me, and I said, "Honest, it's not my fault!" They laughed, and someone said, "It's not ours either, Ma'am." We still had three hours left. We started conversing. One staff sergeant said, "Ma'am, I remember every time an officer ignored my advice because I'm black." A master sergeant told me, "Ma'am, I remember every time a white soldier got credit for my good work." A sergeant major looked me in the eyes and said, "Ma'am, I remember every time I was called nigger in uniform." Wow. I have to admit that, at the end of three hours, we had not solved racism.

I realized how futile it was to assign the problem to those who were the victims. It required a top-down, culture-wide change in attitude. At the end of the three hours, I wrote a report to confirm that racism was a problem throughout South Korea and that the recommended solutions included educating the commanders and holding them accountable. I don't think the report went anywhere, but I walked out a better leader. When I was about to leave, the sergeant major said to me, "Ma'am, you are an officer; you have the power. Please treat all soldiers—black, white, and brown—fairly, and with dignity and respect." I promised I would.

Many bosses will not admit they need help because they fear it will undermine their authority. Direct reports may be uncomfortable asking for help because they fear the boss will assume that they are not up to the job. These fears can cause damage to the organization and to your reputation.

As a leader, you need to be comfortable turning to others for assistance. After trying to fix a problem without success, I had to make three decisions: I had to decide what support was needed, who could help me best—boss, colleague, or an expert—and what options for possible solutions I would bring to the meeting.

I armed myself with different options to take to the boss to show that I was serious about trying to solve the problem. Do not go empty-handed when you seek help. Show that you have carefully thought through the issue. You are not asking for someone else to take over the job; you are there to work together on the problem. When you present options, you are enabling your boss to look at the problem, assess your ideas, and, if necessary, come up with her own resolution. Instead of asking to be rescued, you have created a collaborative brainstorming opportunity with someone in authority.

Asking for assistance can be a strategic move for you. You have shown that you won't let pride hurt the organization and are humble enough to seek help.

As a leader, when someone comes to you with a problem, have her bring possible solutions. This is a learning opportunity for her to develop problem-solving skills. When an answer is found, if possible, delegate the implementation to the person who brought you the issue. This will encourage her to take ownership and have a sense of accomplishment.

EVERYONE IS FAKING IT

Remember that you're in very good company if you feel like you're just faking it. A tremendous number of successful people feel that way. When you feel insecure in your role as a leader, try a little playacting. Channel your inner child or actress and throw yourself into your "role" completely without self-doubt, fear, or lack of confidence. Project confidence on the outside even if you don't feel it inside. In the DMZ, I playacted at being a soldier and a leader until I began to grow into the role and gain enough confidence to embrace it for real. I now know I'm not the only leader who feels insecure at times.

4

LEAVE NO ONE BEHIND

In May 1978, the Army promoted me to first lieutenant. It was amazing how the change from a gold bar to a silver bar (in the military, gold is lower than silver because gold represents the ground and silver the stars) led soldiers to show respect.

Napoleon said, "An army marches on its stomach," meaning soldiers need to be fed and housed to be effective. As an executive officer for a headquarters company responsible for feeding, training, and housing several hundred soldiers, I can attest to the truth of this statement. I handled all the reports for the military intelligence brigade regarding personnel, vehicles, and weapons. In other words, I was responsible for the often thankless job of keeping soldiers fed, warm, and ready for combat. For this, I relied on my three best soldiers, who happened to be women.

Karen, Tonya, and LaJoyce were efficient, positive, and thorough. Under their supervision, we kept winning awards for best supply room, best arms room, and best motor pool. Sometimes, they would visit me in my office at the end of the day to let me know what was happening around headquarters, what the enlisted personnel were concerned with, what people were praising or complaining about. Often we just chatted.

One day, Tonya called and asked if I could meet with them after work but asked me not to tell anyone. I showed up at the office and sat them down. "What's wrong?" I asked.

"Criminal Investigation Division is trying to prove we're lesbians and kick us out of the Army and give us dishonorable discharges," Tonya said, her voice shaking.

I said, "Don't worry. I'll call CID and straighten this out."

Tonya looked at me. "That's the problem. We *are* lesbians."

I was in a real quandary. What they did not know was that months earlier, the colonel who commanded the brigade had called me into his office and told me, "We have lesbians in this unit. I want you to hunt them down and kick them out." I was stunned by the order. I had joined the Army to hunt down communists, not lesbians. After I got the order, I had gone back to my office and looked up the offense in the Uniform Code of Military Justice—the military law book. Gays and lesbians in the military, before the "Don't Ask, Don' Tell" edict of 1993, faced court-martials, felony convictions, dishonorable discharges, no military benefits, no federal jobs, and no GI bill.

As I looked at these scared soldiers, I decided to disobey an order—but I knew it was the right thing to do. I went through the military law book and showed them how the military would try to come after them. I said, "No matter what, you cannot admit to being lesbians."

Those three took my advice and successfully stayed in, doing great service for the Army, and when they left, it was on their own terms. That day, I kept the promises that I had made to Sergeant

Sampson from boot camp and the sergeant major from South Korea. Both of these men had reminded me that I had the power to take care of all soldiers, and I had said I would.

Part of the empathy I felt for the three women stemmed from my own experience of being marginalized. In 1969, my father went to war and my family moved to New England. We showed up with our southern accents in a northern all-white town. It was strange because my sister and I, both white, were subjected to racist remarks. Because of our southern accents, the kids and some of the teachers in the junior high school treated us as if we were stupid, and the kids had a blast making up insulting nicknames for us. I was Aunt Jemima. My sister had it worse: she was Buckwheat. To prove we were not stupid white trash, my sister and I really buckled down in school. We worked harder than the rest to overcome

PEOPLE BEFORE POLICY

Leaders put people before policy. Many fellow officers were shocked when I told them that I had disregarded an order. Throughout their military service, they had parroted the words "Mission first, people always" but chose to ignore those words when someone was different. As a band of brothers and sisters, we stayed focused on the mission while watching out for each other. I put "Mission first, people always" into action by protecting the women. The commander who had ordered me to hunt them down was not focusing on the missions of pursuing the enemy and taking care of soldiers. As a leader, you have a responsibility to question policies that harm people.

the stereotypes. Looking back, I see how this experience made me a better leader. I became sensitive to bigotry. I became committed to leaving no one behind, regardless of race, gender, religion, sexual orientation, and so on.

DEALING WITH WEAKNESSES

Leaving no one behind doesn't mean tolerating incompetence, but sometimes you just have to give people a chance to figure out how they can best contribute. In fact, one of the most important traits you can demonstrate as a leader is to know the people you work with. I don't mean prying into their personal lives; I mean understanding what motivates them, why they work, and what talents they bring.

I learned this lesson from a young soldier in my command whose nickname was Peewee. Peewee was a troublemaker: he played pranks on people, goofed off, and generally tried to avoid doing his job. The office phone system allowed us to transfer internal calls. One afternoon, Peewee called the first sergeant in the motor pool and then immediately transferred him to me. We both answered the phone expecting the other to talk first. "What do you want, Ma'am?" "I don't want anything. Why did you call me?" I could hear Peewee laughing loudly in the background.

Another time, he and I were walking to I Corps headquarters. We passed the Corps command sergeant major, who gave me a sharp salute. Peewee said, "Hi, Top." I was horrified. One addressed a first sergeant as Top, not the command sergeant major two levels higher at the top of the enlisted ranks. The command sergeant major stopped in his tracks and said, "Ma'am, I need to speak with this young soldier. He'll be a while." I said, "Hooah" and walked away. Half an hour later, Peewee showed up looking very chagrined. He mumbled something about how he should have called him "Big Top."

How do you handle a problem like Peewee?

One day the first sergeant came to me and said, "Ma'am, we've got a request from headquarters, and I want to give it to Peewee."

"What's the assignment?"

"Headquarters would like a team to monitor the communications between the U.S. Army and the Republic of Korea Army during the war game to ensure that secrets are not being leaked. I recommend Peewee lead the team."

I gave him a funny look. "First Sergeant, we can't put a clown in charge of such a sensitive mission."

"I know," the first sergeant said. "Let's give him a chance."

Against my instincts, we assigned the project to Peewee, and he suddenly became serious and responsible. Peewee impressed us with how well he handled it. That's when I realized something about Peewee: he was a brilliant soldier, but when he was bored, he got in trouble.

From then on, I made sure Peewee was never bored. That is part of your responsibility when you take over a team. You can't always choose your team members. Often you will inherit a team. You have the responsibility to get to know the team members, understand their abilities and passions, and direct them to the fullest benefit of your team.

People will frequently live up or down to your expectations of them. When you label people troublemakers, or lazy, or irresponsible, and you don't outright fire them, then they learn that this is what they can get away with and how they are expected to behave.

Just like children, many adults will push the boundaries and slack off if they know you don't expect much of them. Change up the script, though, and you may find qualities in your workers that you didn't expect at all, like we found in Peewee.

Use language that empowers the worker: "I have a challenging assignment for you, but I know you can handle it." "We could really use a creative mind like yours on this project, which is why I'm putting you on this team." "You're such a fast worker that I know you can get this done for us today. It'll help so much." Even if you're not sure you fully believe it, pick up on what you hope are the person's best attributes and praise those.

Even in seemingly menial fields, there can be pride in a job well done. A friend of mine worked as a bus girl in two restaurants in college. At the first restaurant, she was never praised, and the only time her bosses spoke with her was to correct the way she was holding a tray or to tell her to go back to a table faster. At the second restaurant, the manager told her right away, "Oh, it's so good to finally have an experienced bus girl here! I can see you know what you're doing and you're right on top of things." It made my friend want to work faster and harder to make sure her tables were perfect. After all, that's what someone expected of her—she liked hearing that she was doing a good job and wanted to prove that manager right, so she picked up her game.

ALWAYS AIM TO BE HELPFUL

As a leader, if you see a group of people marginalized, do your best to help them. One day, several older women soldiers showed up at my office. They did not work for me but for an aeronautic battalion down the street. They had sought me out because a male company commander wasn't willing to help them out. They came to me because I was a woman officer. I asked them what I could do for them. A staff sergeant said, "Ma'am, we can't get promoted."

I asked, "Why not? Each one of you has an excellent reputation."

The staff sergeant explained, "Ma'am, we are all WACs. When we went through basic training, the Army didn't let us fire weapons. Now the promotion board requires that everyone be qualified on the M-16. We asked the headquarters company commander to arrange for weapons training, but he denied the request, telling us we had to wait for the annual training. The promotion board meets before then. We're in a real bind. Can you help us?"

I looked at these good soldiers who were about to be outranked by their male peers simply because they had never fired the M-16 rifle. If they had come to me sooner, I could have fit them into the military intelligence company annual weapons firing. The easy thing to do was tell them it was outside my purview and they needed to work through their chain of command, but I realized that was the slow and not necessarily successful route. My father had told me that a leader fights for the team. These women weren't in my command, but they were part of the Army team. I couldn't leave them behind. Although I wasn't yet sure how I would negotiate, I knew I had some contacts who might come in handy, so I told them I would fix the problem.

After they left, I went into my supply room and inventoried the canisters of CS gas—tear gas. For some reason, those canisters were not on the property book. The first sergeant and I had discussed how we did not need them, but we did not know what to do with them. Now I had an idea for how to use them. I called the Special Forces unit in another town, where they ran a firing range six days a week.

"I have some women who are in a bit of a predicament," I said to the training NCO. I explained the problem and asked if I could bring a busload of women to his firing range. Then I offered the tear gas as an incentive. Looking back, maybe I didn't need the tear gas. Maybe a busload of women was enough. He agreed to train and qualify them later that same week.

I requisitioned a bus and bus driver. Three days later, 30 former WACs and I drove to Berchtesgaden. The bus parked, and I disembarked. I asked one soldier where I would find the training NCO. He pointed the way. As I walked away, he took off his green beret and snapped it on my butt. *Are you kidding me?*

With fire in my eyes, I turned around, ready to go ballistic on him. Then I saw the bus with 30 women's careers on the line. I decided to pick my battle. Chewing him out was not worth it. I turned back and walked into the training NCO's office. That day, 30 women were able to advance their careers.

Too often, people are marginalized because a manager thinks he or she knows everything about them. One day, a male major from the Pentagon showed up at the headquarters to collect data and information on problems women were facing in the military. I welcomed his visit. I was thrilled that the Pentagon was taking an interest in the issues challenging women. If anyone could improve the situation, it would be someone from the Pentagon. I arranged to have as many women soldiers in the room as possible to share their issues with him.

But it didn't go as I'd hoped. Every time a woman would bring up a problem, such as the uniforms issued to them were too big and tailoring wasn't available, or how men got to take time off for a haircut but women weren't allowed to, he would belittle it and say it was not a "real" problem. He kept repeating that he had a daughter, so he knew what was best for us. Somehow she represented every one of us in his mind—he thought that if he understood one young woman, he must understand all of us. As I watched the women get angry at his lack of listening and empathy, and as I heard him say for the umpteenth time that he had a daughter and therefore knew best, I finally asked, "Sir, is your daughter in the military?" He was taken aback. "No."

"Then, sir, how is it relevant that you have a daughter?"

The meeting was a fiasco. The women left more frustrated than when they arrived. As leaders, we cannot lump people into categories. We must strive to learn what their individual needs, passions, and talents are.

A true leader is inclusive, not exclusive. Everyone has a chance to contribute and to advance. A leader watches out for the vulnerable employees. Vulnerable employees include women, racial minorities, foreigners, the LGBTQ community (lesbian, gay, bisexual, transgendered, and queer or questioning), the disabled, veterans, seniors, millennials, administrative support, introverts, and anyone else who does not resemble those in power. People are left behind when their achievements are ignored or when they do not receive equal pay for equal work, do not receive promotions, are not invited to power events, or are not mentored, coached, championed, or sponsored. People are left behind when they have no voice in contributing solutions, their ideas are belittled, and they are treated with disrespect that includes name-calling, offensive pictures and signs around the workplace, and inappropriate humor.

Leaders must approach diversity with management commitment, training, education, and networking opportunities. As Pat Harris, global diversity chief of McDonald's explains, "The real secret of our success has been the constant application of these

name. This really does matter to people—using their names makes them feel recognized and "seen" as a person, which can improve morale significantly.

Introduce your employees to each other and to superiors. Take employees with you to important meetings. They will be honored and know they are seen.

Tell them what is in it for them. Don't wait until someone is looking to leave. Promotions and money aren't the only answer, so ask how you can make the job better. Then show the valued player the options. Research has shown that employees value the following:

- Career growth

- Exciting and meaningful work (especially millennials)

- A great team

- An inspiring leader

- Humor and fun

- Independence over work

- Fair pay and benefits

- Learning and training opportunities

- The best tools and technology

- A family-friendly workplace

- Job security

Express appreciation. Be glad you have your employees and tell them so, in the form of words, birthday or holiday cards, thoughtful notes, and so on.

As a leader, how do you love that unlovable employee? She irks you. He pushes your buttons. It's her personality. It's his work habits. You can't like all the people you work with, but you can respect them. The challenge is to see the benefit each of these individuals brings to the team while consciously making sure you treat each one fairly.

5

CHARM IS A VERB

Many of my leadership lessons came from my dad; however, one important lesson I learned came from my mother, who would say, "Charm is a verb." She taught me that charm doesn't hinge on being pretty or amusing but rather comes from actively listening to others and genuinely being interested in what they have to say. In business, any leader who doesn't devote time to listening to frontline staff or customers is missing out on valuable intelligence.

I learned the value of this lesson on assignment in West Berlin. After World War II, Germany was divided in half, with West Germany a democracy and East Germany a communist state. West Berlin was democratic and overseen by the Allied forces. I was awarded the World War II occupation medal for my service in Berlin, as American, British, and French forces were considered occupational forces. East Berlin was communist and overseen by Soviet forces. Further to the east in the Soviet Bloc were communist Poland and the Soviet Union. To reach West Berlin from West

Germany, one had to travel through a series of Soviet-controlled checkpoints in East Germany.

The Soviet Bloc and Allied forces could travel between the split sectors of Berlin. When Allied forces visited the East, we were required to be in uniform. I occasionally went to East Berlin for the ballet. Going through Checkpoint Charlie was unnerving because you had to traverse barbed wire, German shepherds, tank traps, and East German soldiers armed to the teeth. East Berlin was shockingly poor compared to West Berlin. The apartments were monolithic gray buildings, and people had to line up to buy anything.

In 1980, the Army promoted me to captain. Despite tensions on the outside, I felt at ease commanding my unit. Most of the soldiers stationed in West Berlin were the top of their respective schools. We all worked hard because the threat was just over the wall. Everyone had a sense of the importance of the mission. I also attribute our success to my first sergeant, who instilled within each person the importance of his or her skills, tasks, and the operations. He taught me to take the time throughout the month to speak with the soldiers individually, to remember their children's names, to ask about their parents, and to say, "I appreciate what you're doing."

The "small talk" that I made with my staff paid off in a very visible way. The Soviets and East Germans were using every means at hand—spies, satellites, and listening posts—to gather intelligence against the Allied forces. During this time, I developed a ritual of going home at lunch to walk my Labrador-mix puppy, Beauregard, eat a sandwich, relax on my front stoop, and chat with whoever came by. One day I bumped into a lieutenant and a captain sitting on my stoop. The lieutenant managed the post office. "Do you want any Soviet souvenirs?" he asked.

I laughed and said, "No, thank you, I have enough belt buckles." When we went through the checkpoints to go through East Germany to get to the western side, if you placed a *Playboy* magazine on your windshield, the Soviets would take it and leave you a belt buckle.

"I'm not talking about belt buckles. I can get you anything," he insisted.

"You can really get me anything?"

"I can get you Soviet fur hats and fur coats."

"What else can you get me?" I said.

"I can get you antiques that the Germans took from the Turks and the Greeks."

My antennae went up. "Really?"

"I can get you paintings. I can get you wined and dined in East Berlin, to the symphony, and to the orchestra."

I thought, *What do the Soviets want from the lieutenant? He doesn't know military operations.* Finally he said, "Well, they're going to give my brother a tour of Eastern Europe—you know, Czechoslovakia and Poland."

"What does your brother do?"

"He's a satellite engineer in Sunnyvale, California."

Bingo.

"Really? Oh my gosh. Do you see what time it is? I have got to get back to work. I'll see you later," I said, emphasizing the *you*, and waved goodbye.

As soon as I got out of line of sight, I dashed to the headquarters, ran up the stairs, and burst into the operations security colonel's office.

"You are not going to believe what the Soviets are doing," I said to the colonel.

"Captain Morgenthaler, calm down. What are the Soviets doing?"

"They are about to kidnap an American satellite engineer."

The colonel was on the phone immediately. That afternoon, military intelligence brought in the lieutenant to learn everything he knew and to protect his brother.

Rapport is necessary to be a successful leader. To build rapport, you must listen. I mean really listen, not be distracted by the fight you had with your spouse that morning or thoughts about your to-do list. Charm is the art of listening. As with any other art such as singing or painting, the more you practice, the better you will become.

SHOWING YOUR OTHER SIDES

Charm also means showing your people you can relax and join in. For fun, the German-American club decided to hold a cake-baking contest to see if Germans or Americans were the better bakers. I could have ignored the contest because I had many other important things to occupy my time, but I decided to enter and made a chocolate rum cheesecake. When the head judge announced me as the winner, I came up for my award. The Germans were surprised to see that the winner was a captain—and a female at that. They had not met a female captain before. As I was handed the blue ribbon, I asked if I could have the rest of the cheesecake for my friends. The judging panel looked sheepish and admitted they had eaten the whole cake.

Experiences like this allowed my team to see me as a whole person, not just "the boss."

Do you remember being a child and seeing your teacher around town in the grocery store or mall? For many kids, it's exciting and bewildering: *You mean teachers are regular people who shop in stores, too?* It's hard for kids to imagine that teachers don't live at the school and spend all their free time on lesson plans. It can be doubly exciting to see them doing things unrelated to their normal positions of authority—like a teachers-versus-students basketball game or a staff talent show.

We don't altogether lose that feeling as adults. Seeing the boss in a more human light can be exciting, too. Workers may see just one side of us and not imagine that we have other hobbies, interests, or talents.

If you are able, plan times when the people on your team can cut loose and show off their other interests—anything from a company bowling night to an impromptu concert.

INVESTING PERSONAL TIME

I invested personal time in teaching soldiers skills that were not necessarily job related. One such soldier was Buddha, the top-ranking sergeant in my command in West Berlin. He had grown up in the inner city and had no opportunity to learn to swim. Having no experience, he had a phobia of the water. However, once he had children, he knew he had to get over his phobia. His children grew up swimming, as they lived on military bases around the world. Buddha knew that I spent my free time teaching disabled children how to swim, and one day he asked me if I could teach him. I had never taught an adult and told him so, wondering if he'd be better off taking a formal class. He said, "My biggest fear isn't water; it's not being able to save my children. I don't want my family to know what I'm up to until I can dive and swim across the pool."

So we secretly met at the pool, and he threw himself into it (pun intended). It wasn't easy. Buddha was all muscle. He had to hold onto three kickboards to stay afloat. First, he learned to breathe, then float, then stroke. We kept the lessons in small, doable chunks. One evening, he brought his kids to the pool. They were playing in the shallow end when he hollered for their attention. From the deep end, he executed a dive and swam the length of the pool. The children started cheering, and everyone applauded as he climbed out with a great smile on his face. It felt terrific to be able to help someone like this, and it established a great rapport between us.

Think about what skills you can put to good use to help your team. Don't be shy about sharing your talents. Find ways to offer your help, and you may find that your team will reciprocate.

ACTIVE LISTENING

One of the more charismatic leaders I met was an undercover police officer with the West Berlin police. He had taken it upon himself to show me the spy games going on between the East and the West. As he was teaching me, he had the ability to make me feel like I was the only one who counted. He listened carefully and never mocked my questions. Many people in West Berlin believed that every third person was a spy, and David took it upon himself to show me it was true. Sometimes I felt like I was caught in a *Mad* magazine *Spy vs. Spy* comic strip. He asked me if I wanted to join him at a terrorist bar one evening, and I jumped at the chance.

"What do I wear to a terrorist bar?" It was 1979, so I chose the Annie Hall look: silk blouse with a tie and tweed pants. With my short blonde hair and that outfit, I screamed American. He picked me up, looked at the outfit, and noted that I was about as American as apple pie à la mode. We entered a seedy bar, and I stood out. Soon, David was working the room, giving each person his undivided attention, actively listening and gleaning important information. As for me, I was fighting off the creepy men. After a while, I decided David had plenty of information and gave him the "let's get out of here" look. As he drove me home, he pointed out that you never know who might have essential information. Speaking to people outside your inner circle might give you powerful insight into the competition, the marketplace, morale, or future operations.

Here are some techniques to improve your listening skills:

1. **Stay focused.** Put down the smartphone; turn away from the computer. Look directly at the speaker. Listen and observe nonverbal body language. Don't start thinking about what you're going to say. Stay focused.

2. **Show that you are paying attention.** You do this through your body language (leaning forward and keeping an open body posture, not crossing your arms or putting your hands in your pockets, and nodding) and by saying "yes" or "please continue."

3. **Reflect aloud what was said.** Paraphrase what you think you understood. Ask questions to clarify. Repeat points made. Summarize the speaker's comments periodically.

4. **Don't interrupt.** Do not try to finish the speaker's thoughts.

5. **Let the speaker finish each point before asking questions.**

6. **Respond respectfully.** Be honest in your response and respectful in the way you answer. Present your opinions calmly and assertively.

7. **Practice.** When I'm with friends or family, I remind myself to simply shut up. Then I actively listen.

BE ACCESSIBLE

Great leaders are accessible. It is assumed that the higher the position, the less accessible the leader. In General Colin Powell's book *It Worked for Me: In Life and Leadership*, the general shares a story about speaking to the parking attendants at the U.S. State Department. Because the garage was so small, the attendants had to "stack" the cars one behind another. At the end of the day, when everyone was trying to rush home, people had to wait for the cars to be pulled in and out. One day, General Powell asked the parking attendants, "When the cars come in every morning, how do you decide who ends up first to get out, and who ends up second and third?" They gave each other knowing looks and little smiles. "Mr. Secretary," one of them said, "it kind of goes like this. When you drive in, if you lower the window, look out, smile, and you know our name, or you say, 'Good morning, how are you?' or something like that, you're number one to get out. But if you just look straight ahead and don't show you even know us or that we are doing something for you, well, you are likely to be one of the last to get out."

Ways to be an accessible leader include:

- Truly have an open door, so people are comfortable engaging with you.

- Meet and get to know the top 20 percent of the organization. Invest in their success.

- Get to know the people who cross your path every day: parking garage attendants, administrative assistants, security guards, IT support personnel. Invest in their success.

- Share information.

- Push down awards. Make sure the receptionist has as good a chance as the top salesperson to be named employee of the month.

- Mentor and champion employees from each level of the organization, not just the senior echelons.

SHOW YOU CARE

A leader not only respects the members of the team but also cares for them. Here are ways to show you care.

- **Know the individual.** Remember details about each person's personal life. If this doesn't come naturally for you, write things down—remind yourself that Mike told you he's going for heart testing next week, or that Kristy told you she's going to visit her ailing grandfather out of state this weekend. Follow up and ask questions: "Did you get your results yet?" "How was your visit with your grandfather?"

- **Appreciate instead of thank.** Visit teams and direct reports when you can. Make the time. Say "I appreciate what you are doing." This is much more powerful than "Thank you."

- **Offer training.** It can be relevant to individuals' current position, it can prepare them for the next level, or it can simply enhance their personal development.

Learning how to use charm can make people open up to you, trust you, and feel appreciated and recognized, all of which can contribute to a better work environment.

6

Facing Fear

As a leader, you are almost certain to face some scary situations. You don't have the benefit of letting others come up with plans or make decisions; you're the one who needs to shoulder much of the burden. In the military, that's often life-or-death stuff, which comes not only with the fear of your own mortality, but with the profound responsibility for other people's lives, too. But even at relatively cushy desk jobs, a leader has to face other sorts of fears—the fear that the company will get sued or go bankrupt, the fear of launching a new product that may fail, the fear of public speaking, even the fear of success.

People have missed out on job promotions because they were afraid of greater responsibility—and the accompanying account-ability—or were simply too scared to ask for it. When it comes to dealing with the "big" fears, it can be helpful to tackle smaller fears first and gain the experience: "Oh, *this* is what it's like to conquer a fear." That's what I did in Hawaii.

During the summer between my two years of graduate school, I taught military intelligence at the Sixth Army Intelligence School in Long Beach, California, alongside 20 other intelligence officers. The military intelligence branch officer talked to us about possible wartime assignments, and I got lucky: mine was to Hawaii. My job was to conduct military intelligence operations at U.S. Pacific Command in a possible buildup to war. In preparation, I had to train in Hawaii for several weeks. He cut orders for me to report to Honolulu in August.

I arrived and was pleased to learn that I was working for an Air Force major, an Army colonel, and a Marine general at Camp Smith. During the week, I found an officer who was willing to scuba dive with me on Saturday. I was recently certified in Monterey, California, and only had four ocean dives under my belt. He was a dive master with years of experience. I met him on the beach at 6 a.m. The surf was rough, but he thought that once we swam beyond the rocks, the waves would calm down. We put on our gear, did a buddy check to make sure everything was working, and walked into the surf. Once we were more than waist deep, we gave each other the sign to submerge. Visibility was only a few feet. We headed further out, hoping to gain greater visibility. Instead, it got worse. Blinded by the churning sand, I got disoriented. I didn't know where the shoreline was. I could feel panic developing. I wanted to shoot up to the surface, but I didn't know which way was up. I knew panicking could kill me. My buddy pushed his face up to my mask and signaled for me to hold onto his weight belt. I realized I had to trust a stranger to get me safely back to shore. I grabbed his belt and reminded myself of his training and experience. I knew he wanted to make it out alive, too. I relaxed as he led us out of the water. I chose to trust him instead of letting fear rule me.

When we made it to the beach, we were both strangely exhilarated. He admitted that he had been scared, too. We had had a lousy dive, but we both had beaten our fear.

Conquering fear can be addictive. The rush of pride—and adrenaline—fuels a drive to figure out what *else* you can conquer today.

———

"Fear is the most powerful emotion," according to University of California Los Angeles psychology professor Michael Fanselow.[1]

Having been a child who was afraid of heights, horses, water, strangers, ticks, quicksand, and a myriad of other things, I was fortunate to have parents who did not indulge my fears. My biggest fear was of water for two reasons: First, when I was a little girl, we lived in Hawaii and the waves scared me. I had recurring dreams that they would sweep me away. Second, when I was six, we were stationed at Camp Pendleton and spent a lot of time at the military pool. One day I was playing in the pool with my brother and sisters, and a friendly Marine grabbed me and threw me high up in the air. I hit the water and sank to the bottom. As I looked up, I was terrified that I wouldn't make it back to the surface. Someone plucked me from the pool floor, but the fear of water never left me.

When I was in elementary school in Altoona, Pennsylvania, my father watched me miss out on all the fun of playing at the pool in the summer or in the ocean when we went to visit relatives in New Hampshire. He didn't know the reason for my fears—one doesn't talk about fears with a Marine father—but he was willing to help me overcome my phobia. He went to the Altoona YMCA and asked about swim classes, but the Y didn't offer any. So he found an instructor who would give me private lessons at the Y, and it worked. The lessons gave me confidence and instilled a love of swimming. I later competed on swim teams, became a Red Cross lifeguard and a swim instructor, and am now a master scuba diver. Not bad, considering my start.

Strangely enough, my nightmare of being swept away came to life in Monterey. It was the last day of finals for my master's from Monterey Institute of International Studies. I rose early to run along the ocean. I wanted to be awake and sharp. It was a beautiful day, and I was enjoying the view of Seaside and Monterey, the smell of the ocean, and the morning breeze. As I ran between the ocean and the seawall, a huge wave that I hadn't seen slammed me against the wall and started dragging me into the ocean. My instincts took over, and I scrambled up the seawall. I looked at the ocean, shocked to see such huge waves moving in. I later learned that this was the impact of a tsunami begun by an undersea earthquake.

I was stuck on the narrow seawall. To get back to my car parked at a hotel, I realized I would have to jump down onto the beach and run as fast as I could. I timed the waves. There wasn't enough time between waves to make it to the parking lot, but there was time to make it to the foundation of the hotel. I watched the next huge wave pull out; I jumped on the beach and sprinted with all my strength toward the hotel. I saw the next wave coming, huge and merciless. I raced to the wall of the foundation and threw myself at it. People looked down helplessly at me as the next wave crashed into me and dragged me. I clung to the foundation for dear life, ripping my nails but hanging on. The wave released its grip. As it retreated into the ocean, I sprinted up to the safety of the parking lot. I had sand everywhere, but I lived. My nightmare had come true—and I survived.

FLIGHT, FIGHT, OR FREEZE

Fear has its purpose. It keeps us out of harm's way and plays a vital role in our self-preservation; yet fear holds us back, too. There are three possible responses to fear: flight, fight, or freeze.

If you spot a bear in the woods nearby, you can walk away as quickly and quietly as possible, you can stick around and try to fight it, or you can freeze in place and hope it will not spot you.

A friend of mine froze when he had to take his first shower after an accident. When he was 20 years old, college student Dale Spencer left a party to walk back to his fraternity house. In the dark, he took a shortcut, walking along a railroad track over a bridge suspended high above the ground. He stumbled, slipped, and plummeted to the earth. Dale lay there and could not move his legs. He screamed for help. He waited. He screamed again, but still no one came. He continued screaming until some men finally heard him and came running.

In the hospital, Dale learned that he was partially paralyzed. He shared with me that as the doctors figured out the extent of the damage, as the nurses helped him learn to get around, and as his mother spent the days praying for her son, he fought innumerable fears. He didn't know if he could finish college, hold a job, find a girlfriend, and live independently. In the early days of therapy, one of his biggest fears was that he would never be able to put on his own underwear himself.

He left the hospital after many months and moved home. When he faced taking a shower by himself for the first time, he froze. He had to wheel himself up to the bathtub, turn the water on, and hoist himself into a chair in the shower. But he was terrified that he would slip out of his chair and fall in the shower, and that he would cry for help and no one would hear him (again). Rationally, he knew he had to bathe. Irrationally, he was afraid he would find himself helpless and alone again.

As he sat on his bed and stared at the bathroom, he remembered his physical therapist telling him to break the fear into small pieces. Instead of worrying that he would fall out of the chair in the shower, Dale focused on properly leveraging his body out of bed into the wheelchair. He exclaimed, "Got it!" Then he focused on wheeling himself into the bathroom and turning on the water. "Got it!" He relaxed and enjoyed taking the shower. "Got it!" The fear of falling in the shower was eclipsed by the pride of "Got it!" and the pleasure of the shower.

"Naw, I'm not a hero. All I was was a scared little bunny rabbit trying to hide, trying to survive," said Captain Scott F. O'Grady at a news conference. O'Grady, the first American shot down while enforcing a U.N. air embargo over Bosnia-Herzegovina, told of parachuting from his burning fighter in full view of Bosnians below. In his autobiography, O'Grady admitted to being frightened. His instincts told him to freeze, his face thrust firmly in the dirt as the enemy approached within feet of where he was. The instinct to freeze saved his life. However, he could not let fear rule him. O'Grady had to carefully plan and execute a way of avoiding enemy detection, protecting himself from the elements, and gathering nourishment by subsisting on leaves, ants, and rainwater.[2]

Both Dale and O'Grady would have failed if they hadn't taken the first step *after freezing*. Dale broke his fear into little chunks and then took each step. O'Grady carefully planned and executed. For some, not trying something is their complete response to fear. The fear of failure ranks up there among the most common fears. Its causes range from childhood events to large mistakes we've made in our adult lives. Ironically, the fear of failure can subconsciously undermine your success.

Imagine if the great inventors and pioneers had been so crippled by the fear of failure that they never set out to sea or went beyond a prototype. Imagine a world without cars, the Internet, or telephones. The inventors of all of them took a leap of faith. Many of our country's greatest historical figures were told flat out that they were going to fail—and yet they didn't allow that to govern how they conducted their lives. They pushed on anyway. They didn't freeze or flee—they fought.

> I read a thing that actually says that speaking in front of a crowd is considered the number one fear of the average person. I found that amazing—number two was death! That means, to the average person, if you have to be at a funeral, you would rather be in the casket than doing the eulogy.
>
> —JERRY SEINFELD

First, realize your fear is legitimate to you. What you feel is real, and you must deal with it constructively. When you are flooded with fear, chances are you aren't thinking clearly. Panic and confusion, not to mention a rush of adrenalin, keep you from taking the necessary coping steps. Therefore, you must calm down, physically and emotionally. Calm brings the situation into perspective. Do what soldiers, firefighters, and police officers do when facing an alarming situation: breathe in for four seconds, hold for four, and release for four. Repeat.

Next, it is important to remember that in everything we do, there is always a chance of failure. Facing that chance requires courage and results in a more rewarding life.

You must have the desire to want to overcome the fear. If you don't want to, you won't. I'm still not comfortable with heights, but I use my mantra, "I'm a warrior, not wimp!" when I go mountain climbing.

Once you are thinking clearly, try to imagine the worst-case scenario. Sometimes the worst is legitimate—such as Hurricane Katrina developing into a category 5 hurricane and destroying the

TOXIC SELF-TALK

Learning how to recognize when your self-talk takes a turn for the worse is crucial. When you hear yourself saying, "I can't," or "I don't know," or "What if," a red flag should go up. Instead of telling yourself, "I can't do X," say, "I can't do X *yet*. But I'm working on it." Or if you start wondering, "What if I fail?" you can respond by saying, "Then I'll try again." Doing this transforms a negative situation into an opportunity for growth. In the end, it's about giving yourself a chance.

A good way to become aware of your self-talk is to write it down. When you catch yourself engaging in self-doubt or self-criticism, write down the thought—and then write down your response. It's a bit like having a devil on one shoulder, but a more powerful angel on the other.

levees that were constructed to handle only up to a category 3. But often, the consequences are not as bad as you imagine.

Take the fear and break it into doable pieces. Do the little stuff, and keep moving forward. Expose yourself gradually to your dread. Neuroscience tells us that our brains still run an operating system that can be traced back to our caveman days, and fear is a big part of it. The most effective way to overcome trepidation is to expose yourself gradually to the object of your dread, which can make it seem less potent. Fear never goes away completely, but you can learn to channel fear as a motivation instead of an excuse for inaction.

WAYS TO FACE YOUR FEARS

There is no cookie-cutter approach to overcoming fears, but there are many techniques that have proved effective.

Do the activity with a professional. She or he will get you through it.

Do the activity with a friend. Before a deployment to the Middle East, I was in the Army hospital getting stuck with needles to protect me against every imaginable disease. One young soldier turned to her buddy and told her that she was scared of needles. Her buddy reached out and held her hand.

Use evidence-based reasoning. Let's say your fear is that you will faint in the middle of giving a speech. Ask yourself: Have you *ever* fainted in the middle of a speech before? What are the odds that this will actually happen to you? Remind yourself of all the times you've had to speak in front of people before and *not* fainted.

Make a list—count up the instances. If you find that all the evidence points to this being an unfounded fear, then take confidence in that. If it's a founded fear (maybe you *have* actually fainted during speeches before!), then determine what steps you'll need to take to make it less likely to happen again. Maybe you need to eat a protein-filled breakfast, meditate beforehand, or lean on the podium during your speech.

Hire a life coach. Many people fear success. Will it change their relationship with their family? Will it put too much stress on them? Will they be exposed as a fraud? A good life coach can help you examine what you want and where the fears originate.

Be a contender. I'm very competitive. If I see someone do something that I fear, I just tell myself that if she can do it, so can I. And then I do.

Join a support group. If you have specific phobias or anxieties, find a support group or therapist that specializes in this area.

Force yourself to deal with it. In the Army, we were taught to rappel off 30-foot towers. The first time I stood on the edge of the tower and looked down, I wanted to take off the rappelling equipment and climb back down the ladder. But I realized that I could not let myself fail in front of all the other soldiers. I forced myself to back up and push off the tower.

Remove the option to freeze and fail. As I stood on the seawall, I knew I could not stay there forever. The ocean would soon reach the top of the seawall and pull me under. As afraid as I was, I knew I had to move to survive. Being afraid was real, but freezing in place was not an option.

It's important to realize that we always have a choice: we can choose to be afraid and do nothing, or we can choose to work through the fear and move forward. Set small goals that will build your confidence. Evaluate possible outcomes and develop plans. Think positively; be a warrior in life. Move forward slowly and steadily. Celebrate the small accomplishments, knowing that you are closer to overcoming your fear.

7

STAND UP AND STAND OUT

In 1985, the Army attempted to pay me to do nothing.

As part of the Army Reserves, I had joined the 353rd Psychological Operations Group at the Presidio San Francisco. The unit's mission was devoted to winning the hearts and minds of the populace and psyching out the enemy during wartime. In many ways, psychological operations (PSYOPS) is similar to marketing: develop and deliver a message to convince people to take the desired action. The 353rd focused on the Pacific. I helped develop brochures, leaflets, and slide shows to combat communism in the Far East.

The commander, Lieutenant Colonel Buz Altshuler (who later retired as a major general), called me into his office one day and asked me if I wanted to participate in an operation in Thailand. He knew that I had visited Thailand when I was stationed in South Korea. I grinned broadly and said, "Yes, sir!" He warned me that I would be working with Special Forces and that they might not take too kindly to a woman. I said, "Sir, I believe I can handle it."

He looked at me and said in an instructor voice, "Captain, I don't care what you believe. I just want to hear what you know. Saying 'I believe' can be seen as a sign of weakness."

I nodded and said, "Sir, I can handle it."

"Morgenthaler, I have full faith that you will get the job done."

I was excited about working with both the American and Thai military during Operation Cobra Gold, a three-week exercise. Cobra Gold is the largest Asia-Pacific military exercise. Held in Thailand every year, it is as much an exercise in diplomatic relationship building and peacekeeping as it is in training for combat readiness. I jumped at the chance to interact with counterparts from other countries and prove my diplomacy chops. Little did I know that I would need those skills to work with leaders from my own country.

When I reported to the Special Forces colonel overseeing the American operations of Cobra Gold in Korat, Thailand, the first thing he said was, "What the hell are you doing here?" He made it clear there was no place for a woman in his operations. He looked at the major by his side, who nodded agreement. In front of me, he told the major to make sure that I sat in the back of the open area, in the corner, and was invisible for the next three weeks. I left his office in shock, but I reminded myself that Colonel Altshuler had full faith in me doing my job. I wasn't going to let him down.

Although the commander in essence had ordered me to do nothing, I knew I had to do my job. If I didn't, I would be just as worthless as some of the men believed. It was disheartening to me to have served for nine years, putting my heart and soul into completing mission after mission, and still be ridiculed because I was female. I showed no pain on the outside, but it tore at me on the inside.

Over my nine years of service, the disrespect and disregard for women continued even as it became more subtle. Although it was tiresome at times, I knew I had to do more than the male officers to be considered an equal. One day, the major got wind that I wasn't sitting quietly doing nothing as he was commanded to ensure. I was busy designing programs for commanders to communicate with the populace in the event of war. He called me a "pushy bitch" in front of everyone. He outranked me, so I took it. Inside I was seething because he did it in front of subordinates, essentially giving them permission to dismiss me too. But I wouldn't stop doing my job. I told him with dignity, "Sir, I'm here to do a job, and I'm going to do it." He slammed his fist on my desk, called me more ugly names, and stormed away. I took a deep breath and looked at the other soldiers to see if anyone else was going to challenge me. A wise NCO said, "Gentlemen, you heard the captain. Let's get back to doing our jobs."

I found it interesting that I was called pushy. When a man stated bluntly what he thought, he was praised for being direct. When a woman stated bluntly what she thought, she was called brusque. When a man asked for a raise, he was assertive. When a woman asked for a raise, she was difficult to work with. When a man shared his ideas, he was creative. When a woman did, she was pushy.

The major did not let the matter go. Every day, he confronted me with something. The more the major pushed, the more I pushed back. I refused to be diminished. I took steps to be visible and to be recognized for accomplishing my mission.

HOW TO STAND OUT

In most Broadway musicals, there are leading roles, supporting roles, and the chorus. If you are always concerned with "fitting in," then you'll be forever in the chorus. To get one of the leading roles, you need to be willing to be different. It is challenging to take the risk of standing out, but the rewards can be great.

Stand up for yourself. There will be people throughout your life who would like to see you fail. Calmly and respectfully do your job. Keep your boss and team informed of what you are doing.

Be visible. I kept popping out of the corner to remind everyone I was there and I was working. Take your seat at the table; sit as close to the front as you can. First impressions are often lasting impressions. Too many people try to be invisible. Leaders must be seen. It is very easy to be invisible. I was sent to Fort Leonard Wood, Missouri, to assist the Department of the Army in a Partnership for Peace exercise. NATO troops were conducting joint exercises with American troops. One day, the four-star general who was chairperson of the Joint Chiefs of Staff arrived on scene. I wanted to meet him. Before we fell into formation, I whipped out my lipstick and put it on. All the troops were standing at attention, in formation, in our camouflage battle uniforms. We looked like bush, bush, bush, lipstick, and bush. The general walked over to me and asked me where I was from. We had a brief conversation. Mission accomplished.

Pay attention to your posture. Visual cues often set the scene for how you are treated. Posture is an important factor in how others respond to you. If your mother taught you to stand up straight, she was right.

Walking into a room standing tall and straight with a smile on your face projects confidence and power. Another way to project power is to stand with your legs wider than shoulder-width apart. Have your arms open—not crossed and not in your pockets. Scientifically, standing tall with your legs and arms stretched wide conveys a sense of power and decreases stress. Research at Harvard and Columbia Universities has shown that practicing the "power pose" for a few minutes increases testosterone and lowers cortisol, the stress hormone.[1]

Look forward instead of tilting your head. Head tilting is a positive signal that you are listening and involved, but it can be subconsciously processed as a signal that you are deferring to the other person. Too many head tilts signal submission. To project power and authority, keep your head straight and in a more neutral position. Another reason to keep your head up is to observe subtle changes in someone's face or body language. If you are not focusing on the individual, you may miss cues that you have lost the person's attention, that he or she does not agree with you, or that the person is preparing to argue with you. In situations where you want to maximize your authority, minimize your movements.

Have a calm demeanor. I am a very expressive person and can get very passionate over issues. In the past, when I have been in the presence of men and I became emotional or excited, I was told to calm down. Unwittingly, I had lost credibility. I learned that by being calm and assertive, I could still make my point. A leader is passionate without being out of control. When you appear calm and contained, you appear more powerful.

Trim your hedges. Be aware of your language. Too many "I believe" or "I think" statements can weaken your position. "I think I can," "Well, I guess," and "Maybe we should" are hedges. As a leader, do not hedge. Trim the hedges from your speaking. Also, do not add tags at the end of the sentence that will undermine your statement. The following are tags: "Does that make sense?" "Do you think this will work?" "Right?" Stick to the point, and don't feel the need to request approval.

DON'T WAIT FOR AN INVITATION

Many would-be leaders waste time waiting to be invited to leadership roles. You don't have to wait for an invitation; the more you believe that you already *are* a leader and deserve your spot, the more likely people will treat you that way.

In an interview with AXS Entertainment, comedian Jane Lynch said, "I love this new generation of girls coming up. It sounds so old when I say that, but there's an entitlement to people like Amy Poehler and Tina Fey where they just expect to have a seat at the table, so they have a seat at the table."

Be aware of fillers. Get rid of the "ums," "ahs," and extraneous "likes." These filler words make you seem nervous, defensive, or unprepared. Pause to think out your answer before you speak. Fillers distract and detract.

MAKE THE EXTRA EFFORT

I worked closely with the Thai officers to produce materials they could use if they had to mass-evacuate refugees during a war. Every day during the exercise, I came in with a new Thai word that I had picked up from a local Thai-American newspaper. That was not part of my job description; I didn't have to learn the language or pay attention to the local news, but the Thai military officers were pleased that I was showing an interest in their culture. Many of the U.S. soldiers only showed interest in the strip clubs.

One day, a Thai officer invited two civil affairs officers and me to tour a Cambodian refugee camp. It was heartwarming to see the humane treatment of the refugees. Then he showed us ancient temples and took us into one little village where Westerners had never been before. A toddler saw us, with our white skin, towering over his parents, and he started crying hysterically. Some of the other children would sneak up and touch my uniform. The parents were embarrassed because in Thai culture, it is very rude to touch strangers, but I told them it was fine.

Some of the other officers who had been left behind complained that we got a field trip while they had to do their regular work. I explained that the civil affairs officers and I were the only ones who had showed any interest in the culture of Thailand.

Embrace the cultures you find yourself in or work with. Recognizing the proud history and the beauty of another land makes others warm to you. Don't be the "Ugly American."

Whether in someone else's culture or your own, remember to go above and beyond as often as possible to show that you care not only about your work, but about the people with whom you work. Remembering details about others' lives and preferences can show that you care. Helping to plan a shower for a pregnant employee or showing up at a funeral when someone's family member has passed away can make a big impression, and so can smaller gestures like simply remembering to ask how someone's family is doing, or noting someone's work anniversary ("Hey, you've been working here for two years today—we're glad to have you on the team!"), or remembering someone's favorite type of snack and bringing it in one day.

When you're trying to bond with someone, another good way to do it is to pay attention to what he's into—maybe he's mentioned a favorite TV show, movie, or book, for instance—and then take it as a recommendation.

A week later, you can report back, "I watched that movie you talked about, and you were right—it was really great!"

That gives you something in common, and more important, it shows that you respected his opinion enough to follow it even when you weren't at work. (Just don't go overboard.)

FORGING A PATH

Dealing with the oppressive major made those three weeks in Thailand the longest in my life. I returned stateside exhausted, but I knew I had done everything I could to fulfill my responsibilities.

The next year I returned, and this time I wasn't the only woman soldier. Many had arrived to be part of the mission. This time we were not ignored and were instead assigned meaningful responsibilities. In my "pushy" way, I had made a path for other women.

But pathways are not always smooth. Even after the hardest groundwork is done, you may still have to fight to gain equal footing. Even though I was no longer the only woman in Operation Cobra, I still met resistance to doing my job. I was denied permission to address the one-star general to brief him on our mission.

One day, the four-star commanding general of Special Forces came in from Fort Bragg to see how Operation Cobra Gold was going. When he walked into the room, his aide called everyone to attention. As we stood there, a colonel asked if he would like to be briefed. He said, "No, I want to talk to Captain Morgenthaler." We were all stunned. The men couldn't believe he would want to speak to a woman Reserve soldier. As for me, I still couldn't get over hearing my name and having it pronounced right. I stood taller and said, "Yes, sir?"

He asked me if I knew Colonel Wendell Morgenthaler. "Yes, sir. He's my father."

"Your father was my advisor at the Naval War College. I just had dinner with him and your mother. They are so proud of you."

I didn't know what to say, so I just said, "Yes, sir."

He said, "Keep up the great work, Captain." He then departed.

The next day, the one-star general called me into his office and requested that I brief him the following day on my mission. Thanks to my father, I had access to the leader. Now, I had to show my worth. I prepared a presentation on how the combat forces could use psychological operations as a force multiplier. By using Reserve forces, the commander would be more effective in dealing with displaced civilians and refugees.

The next morning, I entered the war room, greeted the Thai officers in Thai, and took my seat. When it was my turn to brief, I stood tall with the power pose, looked the general in the eye, and discussed my mission. I used the three Bs: be bold, be brief, and be gone. I used assertive language without hedging. I answered his questions succinctly and to the point. When another officer sniped at me, I smiled with confidence and addressed his comment, ignoring the attitude. Inside I was nervous, but outside I was cool and collected. The general thanked me for the briefing and invited me to be part of the morning briefing every day. I was earning my pay.

8

DEALING WITH BULLIES

As a leader, you will almost certainly encounter people who take inappropriate advantage of their power at some point.

In 1991, when I was a major and had served for 15 years, I joyously became pregnant again. My unit was assigned to go to Germany for a three-week exercise that summer, but I was already five months pregnant by then and knew that the Department of the Army did not allow pregnant women to deploy. So I was surprised when the commander came to me and asked me to go anyway. He told me how necessary I was to the mission. I was pleased to be asked; it was flattering to hear that the team needed me. He promised me that I would have a job in a building and not in the field. I agreed.

After buying a larger-size fatigue uniform to mask my pregnant belly, I deployed with the unit to Germany. My quarters and the place where I worked were separated by two tall hills. Each morning, I got up and walked the two miles up and down the hillsides to work, and then, after working a 14-hour day, hiked back. I was exhausted at the end of each day and started feeling that the commander had taken advantage of me; these were longer hours and more physically demanding work than he'd led me to believe. I told myself, though, that it was just for three weeks and I would rest up afterward.

One day the sergeant major told me with concern in his voice that the commander was going to order me into the field.

"The conditions are very dirty, and many soldiers have gotten sick. Some have even been hospitalized," he said. I thanked him for the heads-up.

The commander arrived that afternoon and told me to pack my bags and prepare to deploy to the field. I said, "Yes, sir, as soon as I clear it with the division doctor." Both the commander and I knew I shouldn't be at the exercise. There was no way a doctor would permit a pregnant woman in the field, let alone in a filthy environment. He mumbled, "Never mind" and departed. I wondered if there would be payback. There was.

In December, I had my beautiful daughter and took only one weekend drill off. I could have missed more drills for pregnancy leave, but I chose not to. When I returned in January, I walked into my office and found another major sitting at my desk. I asked him what was up. He told me that he now had my position and that I would work for him.

That was just how he said it—matter-of-fact—and I was expected to accept it.

As I looked at this man who had less experience than I did, I realized that I had to speak to the commander. I went to see him and asked why I had been demoted.

"Don't think of it as a demotion, but as an opportunity to have less stress in life, especially with a new baby," he said.

Inside I boiled. Outwardly, I calmly stated that I didn't require less stress.

"Did my performance result in this demotion?"

"You're misunderstanding," he said. "Again, don't think of it as a demotion. Think of it as a 'compassionate move.'" Perhaps if I hadn't been driven to succeed, I would have appreciated the "compassionate move." To me, it was a slap in my face.

"Sir, is this legal?"

He shot out of his chair and started screaming in my face. As his face reddened, his eyes bulged, and spittle flew, I realized that I had touched a sore point. It wasn't legal. He stood there like the bully I once faced in the playground who tried to push me around. Back then, I had handled it by raising my fists and getting into a fighting stance, and the boy backed down. I couldn't do that with the colonel. I took the screaming. When he stopped, I said, "Yes, sir."

I left his office. I went outside in the January cold to calm down and consider my options. I thought about reporting it, but the "compassionate move" might be persuasive. I thought about transferring out of the unit, which is an option in the Army Reserves. I could begin the search for a unit that would recognize what I had accomplished instead of punishing me for having a child, but I realized that I didn't want to leave. I loved the mission of the civil affairs unit: rebuilding nations. I admired many of the soldiers and officers who were members of the unit. I decided I wanted to stay, but I would not accept the demotion. I would not be in a subordinate role to a less experienced peer.

I thought of possible solutions, and when I came back into the building, I had a plan. I found Colonel Ron Bacci, chief of the economics team, and I asked if I could join his team. He gave me a big smile and a loud "Hooah!" I went back to the commander and asked that instead of the "compassionate move" I would take a lateral transfer. The commander granted my request.

I loved the assignment, and I loved working for Colonel Bacci, a man who understood and respected both parts of my life: my military work and my family life. He exemplified what it means to get to know your team. If I hadn't had the setback of being demoted, I might not have had the opportunity to work for someone better.

FACING SETBACKS

Life has taught me that if you don't take command of your life, someone else will be glad to. You will not like what that person has in store for you. Therefore, when dealing with a setback, take the following steps to regroup and move forward.

Evaluate the situation. What is the problem? Are you facing this alone, or are there others that can band together with you? What is the worst possible thing that can happen to you? How will it impact you in the next year? Five years? This evaluation will help you look at the problem from different perspectives and decide how much energy it is worth devoting to solving it.

Process your emotions so that you can move on. Journaling, meditating, or talking to a trusted friend or advisor will help you calm down and look at the issue rationally.

See the setback as an obstacle that you will turn into an opportunity. Refer to the O.B.S.T.A.C.L.E. approach in Chapter 1 to brainstorm alternative courses of action.

Devise the steps you're going to take. Now, take them.

Learn from the setback.

Celebrate moving forward.

STAND ON A CHAIR

Bullying in the workplace refers to intentional, repeated behavior that is intended to humiliate, embarrass, or degrade an employee. Bosses, supervisors, colleagues, and subordinates can be bullies.

There are times when you may have to literally stand up to a bully.

I attended Command and General Staff College during three summers of my tenure at the 308th. That school is where Army majors go to develop strategic vision and hone leadership skills. The college assigned me as a team leader because of my seniority. Major "Hulk" also led a team. Halfway through the program, the school combined teams, and Major Hulk and his team joined mine. The school kept me in charge because of my seniority (I had made major before he did). He was furious. In front of the whole classroom, with his 225 pounds towering over me, he screamed in my face, "Why the hell are you in charge?"

I resisted the urge to back away. I stood my ground. Over the years, I have met bullies who used their size to try to coerce, and I obviously couldn't compete with him in that respect. Instead, I held up my hand and said calmly, "Please wait." I grabbed a chair, climbed onto it, and, now towering over him, said in a strong voice, "I outrank you by date of rank. Get over it." I stepped off the chair, put it back, and confidently said to the group, "Let's get back to winning the war."

Major Hulk went back to his seat and became a productive team player. We became friends before the end of the program. Facing a bully with confidence is a skill every leader needs to develop. Looking back, I wonder if Major Hulk was aware that he had bullied me or if he was just angry and didn't realize how he was handling it.

Sometimes you need to stand on a chair, metaphorically. Don't let anyone intimidate you due to size, vocal volume, or threatening stance. Do what you can to show that the intimidation is not working: Make sure to watch your body language. Don't shrink down in your chair, wave your hands like a "Nervous Nellie," or look down at the floor. That shows the bully that he's dominating you, which is just what fuels him.

Instead, you need to devise ways to retain your power and dignity.

One soldier came to me to report that she was being bullied by a sergeant whenever she had to work in the motor pool. I asked her to get a soldier she trusted. She brought him into the office, and I requested that they work in the motor pool as a team. If the bully began to taunt her, she was to tell him to stop. The other soldier would act as her witness.

I watched them both head out to the motor pool. Soon enough, I saw the sergeant start to mock her. She stood tall and put her hands out, and I read her lips as she said, "Stop." He laughed. The other soldier took out a notepad and started writing. The sergeant looked surprised, then shut his mouth and walked away.

LEADING WHEN BULLIES ARE A PROBLEM

One of the civilians in the unit intimidated men and women with his size, loud voice, and aggressive behavior. Yet he always complained that no one would help him. People hid when they saw him coming down the hall. Members of the unit made formal complaints, so I was asked to solve the problem. Taking him outside for a fight was not an option. Instead, I sat down with him and explained that by aggressively trying to get his way, he was repelling people.

He was genuinely shocked. He had never seen himself as powerful, or as a bully. I mentored him on listening techniques. He learned to ask instead of demand, and he caught on that thanking someone went a long way. People saw and appreciated the change in his behavior.

As a leader, do not permit bullying. It is destructive to team morale. Putting someone else down is a way for some to hide their own insecurity. And, since you're setting the example, make sure that you do not bully. Ask yourself the following questions: Do you pick on people without power—junior employees, minorities, or women? Do you laugh at people's mistakes? Do you get angry a lot? Do you stay angry? Do you blame others when things go wrong? Correct this behavior by treating everyone with respect.

Bullying may be outright or more subtly orchestrated. I faced one soldier who did not want to work for a woman. He spent much of his time grumbling just out of earshot to every man who would listen about working for a stupid woman. Of course, word got back to me. He also had the foulest mouth; every other word was "f@#king" this, "f@#king" that. This wasn't acceptable language in the workplace. I issued an unusual order that the four-letter "f" word would not be spoken in our section. I told the people in the section that they were smart enough to come up with other, more appropriate words.

The soldier directly challenged me by saying, "I don't give a f@#k what a f@#king woman says." Now he had crossed the line.

The section turned as one to watch my response. I got in his face and yelled in the best drill sergeant style, "I don't give a f@#k what a f@#king woman says either. I give a f@#k what a major says. Got it, soldier?" He mumbled "Yes, Ma'am." I had no more problems with him. Sometimes a bully will back down only when pushed back.

If you are the target, here are steps for you take:

1. **Tell the bully to stop.** This may not be easy. Start by putting your hands up like a police officer to create a barrier. Then say something to the point such as "Stop. I need to work." "Stop the bullying." "Stop the ugly words." Don't escalate by yelling back. This may get you in trouble.

2. **Keep a record of events.** Record the name, the method of the bullying, the time and place, any witnesses, and what was done.

3. **Gather witnesses.** Include those who have seen the bullying or have been victims themselves. Make sure they are willing to corroborate what happened.

4. **Ask for backup.** If bullying occurs in a certain place or at a certain time, have your witness nearby to help.

5. **Speak to your boss.** Do this when you are calm and have collected the evidence.

As the leader:

1. **Put it in writing.** Implement a zero-tolerance bullying policy in writing. The policy should include language emphasizing the purpose of the policy (to prevent workplace bullying and promote mutual respect). It

should contain a clear definition of prohibited bullying behavior and a descriptive list of examples, a statement encouraging employees to report this behavior, a statement that complaints will be investigated and appropriate corrective action will be taken, and a prohibition on retaliation. Clearly state the consequences. Communicate the policy to all employees. Make sure the onboarding of new employees covers the policy.

2. **Tell them you're there to listen.** Have an open-door policy so employees can bring the problem to you.

3. **Investigate all allegations.**

4. **Don't blame the victim.** Be careful; bullies rarely fit the cartoonish stereotype we remember from grade school. They're not all big oafs with no social skills who are secretly jealous of the people they're picking on. More often, they're charismatic and popular—which means they get away with their behaviors, while victims often have lesser social status and may be more prone to getting upset (which is why the bully thinks it's fun). Before punishing both people equally or telling the victim to stop being so sensitive, be absolutely sure that your perception is correct. In many cases, bullies are able to charm their superiors and continue getting away with their bad behavior.

5. **Take action.** If it's corroborated, address the bullying behavior immediately. Bullies are often narcissistic and will not want to change unless it is clearly demonstrated how their behavior will harm them. There must be

consequences expressed in the policy and applied, or the behavior will continue. The consequences can begin with a written entry in the personnel record and end with dismissal.

ONE-UPMANSHIP

As a leader, you will encounter people who will try to usurp your power. I remember working with a peer who believed she was the most brilliant officer the Army had ever seen. She was so good at telling me how to run my staff. I would listen and then politely say, "Thanks for the idea. I'll think on it." She would push back. I would take the next step and diplomatically ask her if I missed something and was she now the boss? She would acknowledge she was not, and I would repeat, "I'll think on it." Being a broken record can be effective, but in this case, even that didn't deter her. She tried this in front of the commander. I turned to the commander and sought clarification: Which one of us was in charge? I got it on the record that I was responsible for my team, not her. That's where it ended.

Another peer loved playing one-upmanship. Whatever I did, he did better. He constantly had to feel superior. If I told a story, he had to top it. I learned to tell my story, let him speak, and then stay quiet—not acknowledging his more exciting addition. Letting the silence drag took some of the steam out of him.

Don't play one-upmanship, the technique of gaining an advantage or feeling of superiority over another person, to constantly feed the need to prove yourself to anyone who will pay attention. As a leader, catch yourself. Listen instead of boasting. The boasts and claims are often a cry for help from an insecure person. Rather than feed into back-and-forth competition, let the next one-up put an end to your conversation.

Employees may seek compensation for bullying behavior under federal, state, and local laws prohibiting discrimination, harassment, and retaliation, as well as under state laws and through workers' compensation.

Once an individual begins to bully, if he or she is not stopped early, the bullying will continue. Let it be known early and often that you are the kind of leader who does not tolerate any sort of bullying. Define it for your team, provide examples, and follow through with consequences. Always set the tone by demonstrating respect yourself.

9

You Have the Power

Even when you've earned a position of power, there may be times when others won't accept it.

A month after receiving the command of the 318th Press Camp, I was promoted to lieutenant colonel. The press camp was deployed to Egypt in support of the United States Third Army for a three-week exercise, and I was assigned to work for a two-star Egyptian general. I was excited to see Egypt and work with the general. Women do not serve in the Egyptian Army, but I was confident that I could make it work based on my experiences serving with other foreign commanders in Thailand and Korea. Nope! I was wrong.

The general was very upset that I was assigned to him. He told me bluntly the moment he met me, "Lieutenant Colonel Morgenthaler, I don't work with women." He looked at my deputy and said, "I will deal with Major Healy instead."

I wasn't angry. I understood that I could not change thousands of years of tradition, but I also knew that the Army had sent me to do a job, and I was going to do it. Plus, my stubbornness kicked in. Tell me I can't do something, and I will find a way to do it.

I realized that as the commander, I could either keep my power or give it away. I decided that I was not going to give away my power.

I told Major Healy that anytime the general made requests to him, he had to bring them to me for my approval. Major Healy was surprised because I am not a micromanager. Usually I empowered my soldiers to do their jobs independently—but not this time. I had to make a point.

My unit and I worked on the bottom floor of a five-story building. The general worked on the top. Did I mention there was no elevator? The English spoken by the general's staff was difficult to understand over the telephone. Therefore, when the general had a mission for the 318th, he would have a corporal run down five stories to fetch Major Healy. The corporal didn't speak English, so he couldn't make the request himself. Instead, Major Healy had to go up five stories with the corporal to find out what the general wanted, and then he had to run down the five stories to get my approval. He then had to run up the five stories again to tell the general that I had approved the mission. Major Healy had the best calves in the Army by the end of our stint.

It doesn't matter what culture you're from; one thing all generals have in common is that they do not like to wait. Finally, one day, the corporal came down and pointed at me to come up to the general. I ran up the five stories knowing that whatever his request was, I would say yes on the spot just for the sake of positive reinforcement. He made his request. I sharply saluted and said, "Yes, we can do the mission."

He was pleased. I was also happy because I had gotten around the gender obstacle, overcome the cultural differences, kept my power, and done my job.

WAYS YOU GIVE AWAY POWER

- You second-guess your decisions.

- You do the task the way someone else recommends even though that is not the way you want to do it.

- You base your decision on what others want, not what the job requires.

- You let others call you names or belittle you.

- You complain but do not fix.

- People easily push your buttons and you overreact.

- You expect the worst from people and from the job.

HOLDING ON TO YOUR POWER

As a leader, you need to set boundaries—whether it's with the power-grabber or the person who refuses to work with you because of his or her biases. If you're starting to feel uncertain, you need to make sure you're acting in an effective way to hold on to your power.

Exercise power early, firmly, and visibly. When you take command, see what decisions are relatively easy to make and make them. Power is the ability to bring about the outcome you desire, so examine what changes can be made for the benefit of the organization. However, don't make change just for change's sake. That can undermine your authority.

Be consistent. When you set a rule, enforce it every time. Don't let some people slide or overlook it sometimes—that just shows others that there are ways to strip you of your power.

Put the power-grabbers in their place. There are tyrants in the office. It may be the guy who claims all the good ideas are his, or it may be the gal who oversteps her authority and tries to dictate to you. Overly ambitious people will work at pushing you out of the picture and into a corner. There are telltale signs of these tyrants. They try to tell you what to do or how to do it. They try to dictate to others who already have enough on their plate without doing their own jobs. They want the recognition without doing the work. If you investigate this, the person might tell you that he's just a great delegator. Or she might tell you she's just looking out for what's best for the company when she means what's best for her. Don't just yes these people to death or ignore them; make it clear that you're in command.

Make things happen. People can easily take power from you if you are not actively engaged in the mission. Sitting on the sidelines or hiding in the office will create a vacuum. Rolling up your sleeves and solving problems, proposing solutions, creating relationships, and improving the organization will get you noticed and respected. Don't blame the economy or funding or staffing for the challenges you face. Just face the challenges.

SEAGULL MANAGERS

At the same time I was dealing with the general, I was dealing with a fellow lieutenant colonel who tried to usurp my command. The Army had turned him down for his own command, so he directed his anger at me. It was evident that he wanted to command the

318th while we were in Egypt. My mission was to assist him but not hand command over to him. He kept trying to circumvent me by giving orders directly to my staff. Worse, he repeatedly counter-manded his own orders, often contradicting what he had said.

He was what I call a "seagull manager": he would fly in, poop on everything, fly away, and leave others (me) with the mess. Within the first three days, everyone was frustrated. I knew I had to fix this fast and with respect. I gave the members of the unit a direct order. No matter what he ordered them to do, their answer would be, "Please clear that with our commander, Lieutenant Colonel Morgenthaler."

The first time a soldier respectfully said that to him, he had a tantrum. He started screaming, "I don't have to clear anything with Morgenthaler. You work for me."

Hearing the noise and expecting this reaction, I stepped into the room and requested that he come into my office. I closed the door and calmly explained how he was wrong. I was the commander. Yes, we worked together, but the soldiers were in my chain of command, not his. He threatened to take it upstairs to the general, his boss. I reached for the phone to make the appointment with the general. Before dialing, I asked, "For clarification, do you really want to tell a general officer that you don't respect the chain of command?"

For the first time, he was silent. I used the break to say that we both wanted the same thing. We wanted to complete the mission with accolades for all. He agreed. We sat down and came up with a way for him to share with me his demands and I would ensure that they were met. If we did not produce results, we would revisit the problem.

I kept him well informed, so he remained comfortable with the solution. With him off their backs, the individuals in the unit per-formed splendidly. The soldiers were happy to do their jobs, and he was happy with the results. The soldier he had screamed at earlier came up to me toward the end of the exercise and said, "I now know why we have officers. You block obstacles so we can do our jobs." His words summarize one of the reasons we have leaders.

As a leader, you have power that can be used in many ways. Use it to remove obstacles for your team.

FIGHTING FOR WHAT YOUR TEAM NEEDS

Some obstacles are the result of our ingrained habits—clinging to outdated modes and ways of doing business because it's how we've always done it. Through research, mentoring, and brainstorming, seek new ways to deal with the impediment. You may have to stop the team and point out how the old way is the wrong way.

Sometimes it means pushing the request up the chain. I realized I had some battles to turn the 318th around. The chief one was getting the soldiers the right equipment to do their mission. In 1996, laptops were scarce—a real luxury in the military. I knew I had to fight to get laptops for the soldier-journalists; they needed them to write stories. I worked with the logistics team, and we made sure we had done all the paperwork correctly to justify the laptops. We were informed that laptops were on the way to the unit. I was pleased because we were preparing for a possible mobilization to Bosnia. But the laptops never arrived.

I investigated and found that Mr. C, a high-ranking civilian in the division headquarters, had confiscated them for his (nonfighting) section. I raised holy hell. Mr. C had cleverly circumvented the system. I lost the skirmish, but both my soldiers and the higher command knew I was not rolling over.

I had to go to Atlanta to brief the Third Army commander on our wartime readiness. A crowd of commanders and sergeant majors from across the Eastern Seaboard filled the auditorium. I was the second-to-last commander to brief because my unit was one of the smallest. All of the commanders before me briefed that everything was fine and they had no needs. I thought, "Really?"

Despite the pressure to act as if everything were fine, I had to take the risk and tell the four-star general the truth. I stood before him and said, "Sir, we are not ready to deploy." Heads snapped up. "The Press Camp does not have laptops." He frowned because this sounded like a frivolous request. I hurriedly explained, "Sir, laptops are to journalists what bullets are to the infantry. The soldiers are out of bullets." The NCOs throughout the room stood up and applauded. They loved that a commander had demanded what the soldiers needed. The general looked at the three-star general in charge of logistics, who nodded.

In fact, he did not just nod; he had the laptops shipped immediately and directly to the unit. The journalists rejoiced. Now they were ready for war or peacetime operations. I couldn't get around the civilian, so I went to the command that would be most affected if we couldn't do our mission.

"TOO NICE" AND "TOO MEAN"

Being too nice or too mean can lose you power. Second Lieutenant "Sweet" came to me one day in tears. She was on her first assignment and was being pushed around by her subordinates. I asked her why she had come to me. She said that she remembered one officer asking me, "Why is a nice Jewish girl like you in the Army?"

I had retorted, "I'm not Jewish and I'm not nice," which she thought was pretty cool.

She noticed that the soldiers listened to me and not to her. As I questioned her, I realized she knew the reason: she was too nice. Lieutenant Sweet admitted that she didn't correct soldiers when they didn't salute her, didn't point out people's mistakes, and didn't address performance problems. She also apologized all the time, even though she had done nothing wrong.

I told her that I could not give her a sugar pill to fix this, but I was willing to mentor her if she wanted to meet with me.

"I'll be up front. Can you handle the frankness?" I asked. She eagerly said she could.

I shared with her that I had learned in commanding in the DMZ in South Korea that I had to use my authority to do what was right instead of nice. I told her how I used humor to make soldiers salute me. I pointed out that as an officer, her goal was to create mutual respect rather than win a popularity contest. She realized that not everyone liked me because I didn't let them slack off; I made them do their jobs. This was a sign that I was a leader, not a friend.

We met in the evenings and brainstormed what she could say or do when someone questioned her authority or, worse yet, ignored her authority. She became comfortable standing up for herself. She heard the "b" word muttered and didn't let it deter her. At lunch one day, I stopped and smiled broadly when I saw Second Lieutenant Sweet outside the Post Exchange store making a private salute her over and over again.

One of the biggest obstacles to holding onto power is being too nice a guy or gal. Too nice can be dangerous. Often it means you are not willing to point out mistakes, address performance problems, or take unpopular but necessary action. Like Lieutenant Sweet, you may find yourself apologizing when it's not your fault. Don't forget, if you say "I'm sorry" all the time, you appear weak and are handing away power. "Sorry" is powerful only when you save it for when you are wrong.

To be a leader, you have to make tough decisions and you must be willing to have difficult conversations. Since leadership is about respect, correct poor performance in a direct way that addresses the problem without denigrating the individual.

You need to be comfortable using your authority to do what is right, even when it's not the "nicest" solution. Think of it like a parent whose kids just want to eat cookies and cupcakes all day; you can be "nice" and give your kid whatever he or she wants, but is that the right thing to do? Of course not; it can lead to obesity and all sorts of health issues. As a leader, you have to be able to see that same bigger picture. In effect, what you're saying is, "No, you can't have another cookie. They're bad for you. Eat this celery instead. You can go ahead and grumble about it, but I'm not going to back down, so you might as well get on the celery train."

If you realize you've become a doormat, you have to change your mindset. You are not there to get along but to show the way. Your goal is to create mutual respect rather than win the popularity contest—to enhance performance, not be best buddies. Accept that no one is universally liked.

On the other hand, being mean will backfire. Many insecure leaders overcompensate with outright meanness. Many years ago before cars had GPS, I got lost in a bad neighborhood in Chicago: there were gangbangers and drug dealers on almost every corner. I made a U-turn, hit a car, and set off the car alarm. I pulled over, and women came streaming out of the apartment buildings. They were hostile until I looked them in the eyes, pointed at the mess I'd made, and said, "My husband's going to kill me!" They laughed, and then shouted at the gangbangers to go away.

I headed to the nearest police station to report the accident. I walked in and explained to the woman police officer what I had done. She started yelling at me because I hadn't brought in the title or insurance card. I was stunned. Here I was admitting that I had done something wrong, and her response was to scream at me. I wanted to say to her, "You don't have to prove yourself to me. I'm a woman in a man's world, too." I realized that her attitude would prevent people from telling her the truth.

Sometimes people are mean. It's a sign that they're frightened, unsure, embarrassed, or defensive. As leaders, we need to curb that. Insecurity causes one to resort to a disproportionate response to a situation. It is neither professional nor respectful behavior.

As Voltaire wrote, "With great power comes great responsibility." There is a reason corruption is so rampant in our government and police force: Power is heady stuff. It can cloud people's judgment and make them feel untouchable, as if the rules don't apply to them. You have to be better than that. Be mindful of the people who let power go to their heads and separate yourself from that. Use your power in the spirit it was intended, to help the company *and* its people.

10

Surprise as a Leadership Tool

There are times in your leadership career when you'll need to do something unexpected or out of character. A slight lack of predictability can work in your favor when you really need to make a statement.

In 1992, war broke out in Bosnia, in the former Yugoslavia. Bosnia imploded with ethnic hatred and genocide—neighbors killing neighbors. United Nations peacekeeping efforts did not end the ethnic cleansing. In 1996, the United States and other NATO nations became involved.

I worked very hard to convince the Pentagon to assign the 318th Press Camp, the public affairs mission in Bosnia, to tell the Army's story of peacekeeping, but the U.S. Army Reserve Command sent a smaller unit, a public affairs company. The main problem was that the major in charge had no active duty experience and no public affairs experience. She had difficulty grasping the mission and taking advice from the experienced NCOs in her unit. She wasn't responding to the mission requests by the higher headquarters. She was not working with the international media to tell the success stories of the peacekeeping operations. The people in her unit were more focused on when they would get to go home for rest and relaxation than on what they could do for the division. The unit under her command performed so poorly that the First Armored commander threatened to ship the whole unit back to the States. If the company had been sent home in disgrace, this would have been a huge black eye for the Army Reserves.

The Army Reserve Command called me at home and asked me to deploy by myself to Bosnia to rescue the unit before it was fired. I called my Reserve commanding general and explained the situation.

"I promise I'll come back a far better press camp commander than when I leave," I said.

He understood the dire situation and granted me permission to deploy.

On my arrival, tensions were still running high as NATO worked to separate the three warring parties: Croatians, Serbians, and Muslims. The hatred seemed counter to the beauty of Bosnia, a country with lush green forests, snow-covered mountains, homes built like chalets, and emerald green rivers. When I traveled through the countryside, it reminded me of Switzerland— except where the genocide had taken place. The atrocities were still evident in different villages. As we convoyed, we would see a house standing untouched while the next was reduced to burnt wood with only the chimneys remaining. Neighbors had turned on neighbors. Friends killed friends. Some villages were destroyed, with nothing remaining except blood and bricks. Armed militias had entered those hamlets, murdered the men and boys, and taken the women and girls to slave camps.

My main mission was to tell Americans and the world what we were doing as peacekeepers in Bosnia. Often the commanding general sent me to troubled areas so that he had eyes on the ground.

One morning, I was the convoy commander for a trip to a military outpost in the heart of Serbian territory. The Serbs had been pulling United Nations workers from their vehicles and beating them. We were under strict orders not to use rest stops or public places. After two hours, however, I realized that the lead vehicle of the convoy was taking us in circles. I had little choice but to instruct our convoy to pull over to the side of the dirt road near a café, even though it was dangerous to stop.

The driver with me radioed the lead, and we learned that the strip map to the outpost was inaccurate. We were lost. I knew we could not sit there too long without inviting trouble; we needed someone to tell us where the compound was. I looked at my driver and declared with humor, "Wait a minute. I'm a woman. I can ask for directions!"

My driver asked, "Do you speak Serbo-Croatian?"

I answered, "No, but I speak a little Russian, and they are similar."

I jumped out of the Humvee, and with purpose, walked into the café. The men sipping coffee and playing chess looked at me with surprise. No one was expecting an American female soldier. Quickly, I said, "Izvinite, gospoda, gde Camp A?" (Excuse me, gentlemen, where is Camp A?)

The owner replied in Russian, "Go east, take the second right, and then three kilometers."

I thanked him and we moved out quickly. Although American convoys were not supposed to stop at public places, I made the command decision to take the risk. I calculated that the element of surprise would be to our advantage, and it was. Sometimes you need to take bold chances and trust that people will be so thrown by the unexpected that they won't have time to react badly.

> A true leader always keeps an element of surprise up his sleeve, which others cannot grasp but which keeps his public excited and breathless.
>
> —CHARLES DE GAULLE

STICKING YOUR NECK OUT

I did something in 1996 that *Defense News* did not publish until 2000. When I asked why the event became public in 2000 and not 1996, I was told that the Army Reserves was not sure that I had done the right thing. But in 2000, another soldier took similar action and the Reserves finally felt OK about it. Here's what was written:

Wherever the Army Reserve is today, from the Balkans to Central America, from an Army Reserve Center in New Hampshire to an exercise at Fort Bliss, Texas, women reservists make their presence felt. Sometimes they do so in rather dramatic fashion, as did Lt. Col. Jill Morgenthaler in Bosnia a couple of years ago.

She took the kind of action that would make any fan of John Wayne or Clint Eastwood—or Sigourney Weaver of the *Alien* movies to use a female action hero—proud.

When a crowd started to turn threateningly toward the deputy commander of the 1st Armored Division, Morgenthaler confronted the leader of the troublemakers. She told him that if he did not calm down his followers, she would shoot him. She did not pull out her pistol. The look in her eyes made it clear that she meant what she said. It convinced the leader of the troublemakers; he ordered the others to back off and the incident ended peacefully.

Perhaps that is not the "traditional" response one might have expected from a woman. Women in the Army Reserve, however, have a way of making their own traditions. They did in the 20th Century and they are doing so in the 21st Century.[1]

Being a woman in a man's world or a man in a woman's world sometimes feels like a disadvantage. However, because it is unexpected and will often surprise others, it can be a benefit. Surprise has always been a military strategy. The introduction of the unexpected causes shock and confusion and can decisively shift the balance of power. By taking advantage of the element of surprise, leaders can achieve success well out of proportion to the effort expended. As people react to someone in a nontraditional role, there is a moment of confusion that gives the leader the opportunity to grab the initiative and be in charge of the moment.

You can use this to your advantage by learning skills that are not expected of you (like learning Chinese so you can speak with big potential clients without a translator, or figuring out what a competitor is up to and secretly developing a better product to come out two weeks earlier). It's also used successfully in advertising, such as with Miracle Whip's "Take a Side" campaign in 2011. It was brilliant because of its unexpected nature: In the commercials, people describe why they love or hate Miracle Whip. We *expect* commercials to describe the love. We do *not* expect them to describe—in unflinching detail—the hate.

"It tastes like lotion, but sweet. And who wants a sweet lotion sandwich?"

"I would rather lick your shoe."

What made it brilliant was that it boosted the company's credibility (it's not pretending everyone loves its product), showed that the company had a sense of humor, and challenged viewers to try Miracle Whip for themselves and figure out which camp they were in.

That's what the power of surprise is about: It throws people off and makes them reconsider their preconceived ideas. Many who had never really thought much about Miracle Whip now wanted to try it just to see whether they'd side with the lovers or the haters. Either way, the company won—the haters still bought the product.

We expect leaders to pretend to be infallible, but sometimes the way you can use surprise in your favor is to acknowledge when something has gone wrong or when you've made a bad decision— preferably using humor to soften it.

BLOWING A KISS

As a woman lieutenant colonel, I was able to use the element of surprise twice to my advantage in Bosnia.

One morning, I was preparing to lead a convoy through a dangerous town. Just the day before, a mob had surrounded United Nations personnel in two SUVs. The vehicles couldn't move. The mob attacked the convoy with rocks and pulled people from the vehicles, severely beating them. NATO forces were under orders to avoid firing on civilians, and yet we had the right to protect ourselves, using deadly force if necessary. As the commander of the convoy, I was determined to keep the soldiers, interpreters, and reporters safe while doing my best to avoid violence against aggressive civilians.

While I explained the task at hand, I could tell that some of the members of the convoy were jittery about driving through this village. Let's admit it: So was I. I didn't want to get beaten up, and I didn't want to kill civilians. I kept my nerves in check as I explained the danger and what our tactics were to get through the village safely, repeating that we would leave no one behind. I sat in the lead Humvee. As we drove through the town swiftly and with purpose, we caught the villagers by surprise. One man ran at me, making a slashing motion at his throat; others followed him with rocks. I blew a kiss at him.

He stopped in his tracks, totally stunned. Everyone with him froze, too. The convoy made it rapidly and safely through.

———

Many villages had stockpiled weapons to protect themselves from outsiders. After the Dayton Peace Accords were signed by the warring parties, rules were in place, especially for the settling of differences through peaceful means. One village violated the accord. As a result, the commanding general ordered a U.S. Army brigade located near the village to seize its weapons. Communications were terrible in war-torn Bosnia, so the commanding general informed me that he wanted me at the brigade command post to be his eyes and ears.

I arrived at the brigade fort too late. The brigade commander had already headed to the armory and was confiscating weapons. I remained in the battle room, listening to the radio transmissions between the fort and the commander. A lieutenant appeared at my side and informed me that four Bosnian colonels wanted to meet with me. I looked at him in surprise. "Me? I don't work here."

"Yes, Ma'am, but you are the highest-ranking officer here."

I looked around, and he was right.

"Oh, and Ma'am, the colonels have with them about 200 villagers, and they're really mad."

I wanted to say again, "I don't work here." Or "Can't someone else do the job?" Or "I'm scared." Instead I said, "Hooah!" I put my bulletproof vest back on, checked that I had my Beretta 9 mm pistol, and headed to the door of the fortress.

As I stepped out of the fort, I was shocked to see that behind the four big Bosnian colonels were villagers armed with two-by-four wood planks and big rocks. I felt like Frankenstein facing the angry crowd. I took a deep breath, stood tall, looked at the sky, smiled upward, and then lowered my head, keeping the smile.

"Gentlemen, I'm pleased to meet you. I'm Colonel Morgenthaler."

The four colonels gaped in amazement. They had never expected a woman colonel to appear. As they stood there stunned, I took advantage of their surprise. "I understand your concerns for your weapons. When you begin to follow the Dayton Peace Accords, we'll be more than happy to return them. I see you have nothing to say, so I'll say goodbye."

I saluted them, turned around, and closed the door to the fort. They remained there briefly and then left, the crowd along with them. That day a woman was the best man for the job.

LAUGHING WHEN YOU'RE EXPECTED
TO SCREAM

It was in Bosnia that I related most to my father. Unfortunately, he had passed away in 1993 from lung cancer, so I was not able to share with him how his leadership lessons were serving me. A convoy of civilian SUVs filled with media personnel and armored Humvees moved up the road on the forested mountainside toward a small Bosnian village in the Zone of Separation (ZOS) where villagers had been killed that morning. Except for the drivers and the gunners on top of the Humvees, the soldiers had dismounted and walked on both sides of the convoy, staying alert. As peacekeepers, we were there to protect the villagers and avoid armed conflict if possible. I saw people flicker through the trees like shadows. I didn't know if they were friends or foes. Paranoia made me especially alert. I felt a fraction of what my father must have felt in the jungles of Vietnam.

One incident I witnessed as a teenager with my father helped me deal calmly with a situation in the ZOS. In 1969, my father returned from the Vietnam War and rejoined us in New Hampshire. As he awaited orders for his next posting, the Marine Corps assigned him to inform the families whose sons had been killed. It took a lot out of him.

To me, he was a hero for serving in Vietnam. To many in society, he was an antihero. One morning, my father had to drive into Boston to meet with Marine recruiters. He asked me if I wanted to come along so that we could catch a ball game afterward. *Cool!* I thought. *Just my dad and me watching the Red Sox.* My father had on his uniform and his medals. He looked so handsome.

After parking the car, we saw that there was a war protest across the street from the recruiting center. A protestor spotted my father, walked up to him, and asked him, "Hey, man, were you wounded over there?"

Dad answered, "Yes, I was."

The protestor then said, "Good. You deserved that, you baby killer!" and then he spat on him.

I cocked my fists, ready to jump into the fray with my dad. As every child of a Marine knows, you do not tug on Superman's cape, and you do not spit on a Marine. What my father did next shocked me. He laughed. The man's demeanor collapsed, and my dad and I walked passed him.

I looked at my dad, puzzled. He said, "I know what you're thinking, but you have to understand that, number one, I am proud of who I am—no one takes that from me. Number two, during the war, I made good out of bad. I saved lives. And, number three, humor is a great weapon. Did you see his face?" We both started laughing together.

In 1996, I learned just how hard it must have been for him to laugh. One day, my team and I were at the edge of a village in the Zone of Separation where atrocities had occurred. The Bosnian Muslims wanted to return and start rebuilding. The Serb militia was threatening to kill anyone who came back. There had been mortars fired and gunshots earlier that day. An elderly man had been killed. We watched as his body was removed from the zone. My team and I stayed in the village assessing the situation and reporting back to the command.

A group of villagers armed with large sticks and stones tried to slip around us into the village. I approached and, with the help of my translator, spoke to the man leading the group. I explained to him that it was too dangerous to return. I told him that once the area was peaceful, NATO would permit them to enter. He threw his head back and spat on me. Seeing me threatened, the soldiers instantly locked and loaded their weapons, aiming them at the villagers.

I look at the spit on my uniform. I thought to myself, "No one is going to die because somebody spat on me." I thought of my father. I looked at the spitter, and I did one of the hardest things I have ever done in my life: I laughed. I pointed at the spit on me and laughed. The spitter looked stunned. The villagers were surprised, and then they started to laugh with me. Tension dissipated. We were no longer the enemy. We were fellow human beings. Once we stopped laughing together, I explained what NATO was doing and why it was still too dangerous for them to return. The villagers listened and left.

One of the best general officers I worked for was General John Abizaid. I watched him treat everyone from the driver to the cook to the combat commander with respect. More than that, he knew who had families, what special interests they had, and what they liked. One afternoon, after a morning of violence in a small town situated in the Zone of Separation, the general and I boarded a Blackhawk helicopter to fly into a hot zone and "get eyes on the ground." As we strapped ourselves in, he turned to his bodyguard, a young corporal, and said, "Isn't today your birthday?"

"Yes, sir!"

General Abizaid reached into his backpack, pulled out a bag of M&Ms, and said, "I believe these are your favorite."

"Sir, yes, sir!" The young man beamed.

Now, this little bag of M&Ms didn't cost much, but it meant so much because the soldier didn't expect the general to know his birthday. This little surprise meant more than the gesture itself. It said, I appreciate you and all that you do. I knew then that I was working with a real leader.

Think about how you can use surprise to your advantage. What would your team not expect of you? What would your rivals not expect? How can you use humor to defuse a bad situation?

11

The Balancing Act

In 1990, Rand McNally offered my husband, Kerry, a cartographer, a position in Illinois. When Kerry and I moved to Illinois with our son, Neal, we knew no one. We left behind Kerry's family on the West Coast and mine on the East Coast and balanced two professional careers with raising our son. We had to find childcare as soon as we could so I could job-hunt. We lucked out. As we were looking at houses to buy in Des Plaines, a woman who was selling her place mentioned that she ran a childcare center for kids from birth to age four. After touring the house, I went to the library and investigated the center. It had a good record. I dropped by the center the next day and was very impressed with the cleanliness, the education level of the staff, and the curriculum for the older toddlers. We had found a gem, and I could go to work with confidence that my child was safe and happy.

In 1991, our daughter, Jamie, was born, and balancing work and family became a little more complicated. When a child got sick, my husband and I took turns using vacation days to care for him or her.

We didn't want either job to suffer. When I went off to the annual Reserve training, my husband bore the brunt of the childrearing. When he traveled to Japan or Holland on business, it was my turn.

In our home, gender roles were not a major concern, and parenting was a joint responsibility. We split the chores. Kerry enjoyed gardening; I killed plants just by looking at them. I handled homework with the kids; Kerry managed bath time. We both did laundry, cooking, and cleaning up. We worked as a team when it came to disciplining the children. We both read and practiced "1-2-3 Magic Parenting,"[1] a method to encourage good behavior and curb disciplinary problems. The kids found it hard to divide and conquer us.

By the summer of 1996, Kerry's sister and family had moved to Illinois, and I had found a wonderful support system with my church, St. Martin Episcopal Church. I left Kerry, Neal (age six), and Jamie (four) to serve for what was supposed to be six months in Bosnia. My deployment was later extended to almost a year. I worried about the impact of them losing their mother. I had never left the children for longer than three weeks for military duty, and military studies have shown that after six months of separation, the fabric of the family begins to unravel. I feared that they would forget they had a mom.

Before I departed, I planned Neal's birthday party. I hired a juggler, wrote the invitations, requested a cake from a friend, and handed the information to Kerry. To remind the children of me for the six months I expected to be gone, I created a paper chain of 180 links, each with a message inside. Every morning, the children read a message. I also arranged for a babysitter for every Saturday, so my husband would have time for himself, to go in to work, or to run errands. My church delivered a hot casserole once a week. Members would take the kids to fun events. I did what I could, knowing that I was off on a grand adventure while Kerry was stuck with the home-work, the bills, the pets, the lawn—everything.

I went to the kids' elementary school and let them know I was being deployed so they could watch for separation anxiety. But the after-school daycare staff was not there when I explained this, and Kerry forgot to tell them why I was absent. When my son mentioned in after-school care that I was a peacekeeper in Bosnia, the staff thought he or my husband had made that up to explain my absence.

Neal did well. He would see me on CNN and tell everyone about me. He was very social and loved striking up conversations with anyone. He discovered that when he wore his T-shirts that said, "My Mum is a Peacekeeper" and "My Mom Wears Combat Boots," adults would ask him about them.

Jamie suffered the most. She was a girly girl who loved playing dress-up and wearing my high heels and makeup. She was always posing like a model. Her ideal Saturday was walking in the mall and window-shopping. She and I had spent a lot of time together, tak-ing mother-daughter jazz class and tap dance lessons while Kerry and Neal did Cub Scouts.

Although she couldn't express it at the age of four, Jamie felt very alone after I left. She started dressing like her brother and father. Kerry couldn't fit in both dance and Cub Scouts, so he brought Jamie to Scouts. By the time I came home, my daughter was dressed in plaid shirts and dungarees. Fortunately, when she could, my sister-in-law would take Jamie out for girl time. A new friend from church who sold cosmetics would have Jamie over to play with the samples. However, when I returned I saw how desper-ately she stayed by my side.

At that time Skype did not exist, e-mail was sporadic, and I was lucky to be able to call home once a week. After six months,

LEADERSHIP ROLES AT HOME

No matter who is more powerful at work, both people in a couple should be on equal footing at home. If you have children, regardless of who is the primary caregiver, you should be careful not to step on each other's toes and contradict each other's parenting styles. Doing so can be very confusing for the kids (who learn which parent can be manipulated more easily) and can shake up a relationship. Trust each other to do what's right.

I started feeling disconnected from my family. I loved them, but I didn't feel a part of them. I felt guilty.

One day, in uniform, I walked down a street in Sarajevo with my eyes focused on the ground. My mind was on my children. I was worried that I was a bad mom, that I was doing long-term harm by being separated from them. I was unsure of the United States and NATO's ability to end hundreds of years of ethnic hatred. I wondered what I was doing there and how this could be worth it. Lost in these thoughts, I felt my hand being lifted, and when I looked up, I saw a little old woman gently kiss my hand. She smiled and walked away. As I watched her, I realized that she was alive because I was there.

I looked around and saw some boys playing basketball. They were finally out of the cellars after four years of hiding because I was there. I grinned when I saw two teenagers flirting on a bridge because I was there. I knew at that moment that I was in the right place at the right time. I knew that my kids were all right. My husband, my sister-in-law, my community, and my church were there for the children.

When I arrived at Fort Benning, I called my husband and told him that I would be home in a few days. We agreed not to tell the children in case the trip was delayed. The kids were in school when I flew into Chicago's O'Hare airport. Kerry picked me up, and we went immediately to the elementary school. I was afraid Jamie would have forgotten what I looked like. When we arrived, the school informed us that the kids were on the playground, so I walked behind the school and looked around. All of a sudden, I heard a little girl scream, "Mommy!" and Jamie charged toward me. I swept her up and started crying. Neal rushed up and grabbed me in a bear hug around my hips.

When I returned home, a local news station did a story of the reunion. They asked Jamie what she had missed most about me, and she said the shopping. They asked Neal, and he said he had forgotten how funny I was.

I spent a lot of time nurturing Jamie. When I would leave a room and forget to tell her, she would freak out. I learned to announce, "I'm going into the kitchen." "I'm in the backyard." Fortunately, time healed her separation anxiety.

LEAVING WORK AT WORK

In 1998, I received the exciting news that I had been selected for the Army War College. This huge honor meant that the Army felt I had the potential to be a strategic leader. In 1999, I began the strenuous long-distance master's program. I had to read piles of books, write many papers, and, two weeks each summer, attend the War College in Pennsylvania. I juggled a full-time civilian job, the Army War College, the Reserve unit, and family life. I got up early every morning to read and write. Saturday mornings, Kerry would take the kids so I could have the whole day to study.

The most challenging part was doing the master's program in the evening while ensuring Jamie and Neal participated in fun activities. Kerry and I agreed that the kids needed to be involved but not overinvolved in activities. Each semester, they chose a fun class. Kerry and Neal also did Scouts. One semester, Jamie was in a dance class and Neal in soccer on different days of the week, and I was having trouble finding the time to study. After I explained my dilemma, the owner of the dance studio gave me her office to work in. While Neal played soccer, I read on the sidelines. At the end of the two-week program each summer at the War College, Kerry put the kids on the plane to me. The children and I toured the East Coast, visiting my mother in Rhode Island before driving back to Illinois. This gave Kerry a needed break.

We made sure the children were interested in the classes they were in; otherwise, the activity became exasperating for everyone. We chose events near home to save time. I made friends with some of the other parents, and we carpooled, giving each of us a break.

Sometimes I found it hard to leave work at work, despite my father's lessons in this regard. At Quantico Marine Corps Base when I was a kid, I watched many Marine officers come home and keep their rank on figuratively. I saw my friends hollered at if they forgot to call their fathers "sir." One day, my dad asked me to do something. I answered, "Yes, sir." He looked at me and said, "Please don't do that. I get enough of that at work. I'm not your sir, I'm your dad." What a relief!

Even with that example, I would sometimes forget and arrive home from Reserve duty as a colonel instead of as a wife and mother. Kerry and the kids would quickly remind me that the eagle stays at the command and the mom comes into the house. I learned to mentally say goodbye to work as I drove out of the parking lot.

MAKING THE SCHEDULE WORK

I worked very hard on balancing my family with work. Too often, a leadership position in the military or corporate America requires putting in long hours, working on weekends, and neglecting vaca-

SWITCHING GEARS

In the car, on the train, or as you walk home, refocus on your family, friends, pets, hobbies, and sports. Here are some suggestions for leaving work stress behind:

- Go to the gym before you head home —get the endorphins flowing.

- Take a longer, different route home (security types will like this one—as we learned in military intelligence, do not take the same route every day to and from your job).

- Listen to your favorite music.

- Scream if you must.

- Make it a rule that you cannot talk about work for more than five minutes a day.

- Make your home your sanctuary.

tions. A friend of mine, Dan, shared with me that serving during wartime was easier on his family than when he was at the Pentagon. When he was overseas, his family understood that he could not be there. His wife got into a routine with the boys. Dan would e-mail and Skype often.

When he returned, he and the family moved to Virginia for his work at the Pentagon. His boys were so excited that Daddy was home and they could make up for the lost time. Unfortunately, Dan's job required him to be on call at all times for crisis management. He told me that it was like a teaser. His kids would see him in the morning, but they never knew if they would see him at night. They would be so disappointed when he didn't come to their Little League games. Dan realized he had to reevaluate his day to give the members of his family what they needed, too.

He revised his schedule to be in the office by 6 a.m. so he could leave at 3 p.m. most days, putting the kids' games on his calendar. He stressed to his staff that those appointments were sacred unless an emergency arose. If he had to go into the office on a Saturday, the boys came with him. They loved being with Dad, and Dan was motivated to get the task done faster. When on a date night with his wife, he put the phone on "do not disturb" mode. If an emergency arose, the duty officer knew to call him twice within three minutes and the call would go through.

LETTING KIDS GROW UP

Some mothers and fathers take parenting too far. One day in Sarajevo, I had an amusing experience with a helicopter parent, someone who is too involved in his or her child's education or career. My phone rang; it was a master sergeant stationed in Germany who was at the end of his rope. He explained, "Ma'am, I have a mother who flew from the States and is demanding to be let on a military flight to Bosnia to check on her son. I can't get her to understand that the situation is still very violent. She can't grasp that peacekeeping operations are for stopping the killings."

I answered, "I'll take it. Put her on the line."

The woman came on the line, identified herself as the mother of a Marine stationed in Sarajevo, and demanded to come into the country. I stared at the phone in horror. The poor young Marine would be humiliated if word got out that Mommy was coming to check on him.

I sternly explained, "Ma'am, your son is an adult. He is a warrior. Every day, violence is occurring. You cannot come into the theater. You cannot see him. Go home."

She tried to interrupt me with her reasons. I asked her, "Do you realize what an embarrassment you would be to your son? Do you realize that you will destroy his reputation and maybe ruin his career because you will not treat him as an adult?"

"Oh, no. That won't happen."

"Oh, yes, it will. Go home."

She continued to argue. When she caught her breath, I told her to put the master sergeant back on the phone. "Take her to the airport!"

I did not track down the Marine to tell him what his mother had tried to do, but he heard it from her. One day, I was informed that a Marine corporal wanted to speak with me. There are 10 ranks between corporal and colonel. It is highly unusual for a corporal to skip the chain of command. I practice an open-door policy, so I had him come into my office.

He stood sharply at attention and said, "Ma'am, I understand that my mother spoke with you, demanding to come into the theater. I apologize for her."

I smiled and said, "No apology necessary."

Balance is the fine art of protecting your children, allowing them to grow up, and letting them go.

CLOCKING OUT

Whether you are married, in a committed relationship, or just hanging with friends, you need balance to recharge. Do not make work-related calls or send texts after hours unless it is an emergency. Put on your personal calendar "rest hours." It can be playing golf, doing yoga, taking a walk in the woods, reading a book, or listening to music. Schedule the downtime and make it sacred on your calendar. Take your vacations. Stay home when you are sick.

Look at your errands. So many women have told me that when they take a day off, they spend it rushing from one errand to another. Can you split the chores with someone else? Offer to do a task that you like for a friend and let her reciprocate with one she likes. My girlfriend picks things up at the store for me, and I return the favor by buying tickets to events online for her.

See who or what might be wasting your time at work. Walk away from the gossips and whiners. Remove the distractions of social media, personal calls, and personal e-mails from work time. Turn off your cell phone until break time or lunchtime. If you get more work done, you may be able to leave early.

You are more than your work. Regardless of your title, you are so much more. List everything you do. Do not forget what you do outside of work, too. Reread it when you are not feeling the love.

As the leader, you set the example for others. Kick them out of the office at the end of the day.

Delegate. Let others grow. Trusting them builds their trust in you. By delegating, you are able to pursue new and creative projects, come up with great solutions, and really walk the walk as a leader.

Have regular breaks. This means taking vacations and coffee breaks. Refresh yourself. Learn to relax. You will be happier and healthier and able to deal with stress better. People want to work for a happy leader.

Emulate balance for your team. Burning out over daily routines hurts the productivity of the team and the organization. A good leader is a balanced leader.

12

Ask for a Promotion
Before You're Ready

There's a danger in getting comfortable: You won't ask for more. The more time you spend picking the low-hanging fruit, the less likely you'll be to stretch yourself and find out what else awaits at the top of the tree.

In 1995, my boss, Army Reserve colonel Ron Bacci, told me about a battalion command position he wanted me to apply for. I jokingly asked him if he was firing me. He said no, but he also told me, "Good leaders push people out when they're ready for the next stage in their development." I have tried to keep this advice in mind throughout my career and in developing my team.

Some bosses take it personally when a person wants to leave for advancement. Luckily, Colonel Bacci wasn't one of them. When I told him I didn't think I was ready for a battalion command, he waved off my concerns. As a banker in his civilian career, he told me how he saw women wait until they were 80 or 90 percent qualified before asking for a promotion, whereas their male counterparts waited until they were only 20 percent ready.

Based on my own experience, those statistics certainly seemed accurate. I had seen a commander give a junior officer a choice assignment that should have gone to me. I was shocked that I didn't get it. I outranked the guy, and I had more experience. At the time, I forced myself to approach the commander and ask why I didn't get the job. He looked surprised and said, "You didn't ask for it." Whoa! Shame on me.

Have you ever wondered why even in a woman-dominated field like public relations the majority of the bosses are men? Women must become more comfortable telling superiors what we want and telling them sooner than we feel we're ready to advance. We must manage the flow of information about accomplishments so that others perceive we are qualified and ready to take the next step.

Asking for a promotion ranks high on the list of professional anxieties. Putting yourself out there is nerve-racking, but think about it: What do you have to lose? At worst, you don't get the job, and even then, you demonstrate to your superiors that you are looking upward.

One of the most important things you can do for your career is to manage its advancement. Too often women leave it up to chance or wait for someone to hand us a promotion based on our achievements and hard work, only to find out that we have lost the job to someone less deserving. But if that other person asked for the job and you didn't, whom can you blame?

Colonel Bacci told me the Army would be the judge of whether I was ready. He gave me the courage to put in my name for consideration to command the 318th Press Camp. A press camp leads companies in handling all aspects of public affairs during war. It is responsible for television, radio, newspapers, and media oper-ations. Even though I had not been a public affairs officer in the Army, my civilian experience qualified me for the position. I reached out to an officer in the brigade overseeing the press camp to see what competition I was facing.

He told me point-blank not to bother with applying.

The command was a plum assignment. Every past commander had made colonel. The commanding general had already let every-one know whom he considered the frontrunner for the position. I decided to go for it anyway.

Two factors worked in my favor: First, I was the only officer who had public affairs experience. Second, the battalion had just flunked its wartime readiness inspection—a real black eye for the unit, the command, and the Army Reserves. As I prepared the letter to the command selection board, I knew I had to show the board how I would remove the pain of failure and turn around the worst press camp. In other words, I had to toot my own horn.

I used what I call the Four S's: self, situation, solution, and suc-cess. Whether you are networking with a power broker, giving an elevator pitch, or enumerating a list of your successes, the Four S's will help you capture your story. I will explain each and then put them together. You should do the same for your accomplishments.

The first S is for *self*. Modesty does not advance your career. You are doing yourself and your organization a disservice by not acknowledging what you have achieved. What have *you* achieved? Often, women and those from certain cultures are uncomfortable talking about what they have done to better an organization. They credit others while downplaying their own role. They couch it in terms of the "team" without mentioning themselves. Some peo-ple even discredit what they have done. "Oh, that's nothing." Self-deprecation will not advance you. You must become comfortable saying "I," "The team and I," or better yet, "I led the team to . . ." You did it, so receive the recognition you deserve.

The second S is for *situation*. What was the problem you solved? Did you help a customer? Did you streamline a process? Did you save money for the company? Did you prevent a crisis? Did you save a life?

The third S is for *solution*. What solution did you, or you and your team, come up with to fix the situation?

The fourth S is for *success*. What was the outcome of your solution? It may be a quantifiable success or a description of how matters improved.

FOUR S'S FOR PROCLAIMING YOUR SUCCESS

You can use this in e-mails, reviews, blogs, public relations, and so on.

Self: What did you do? (*I led the team.*)

Situation: What was the problem or obstacle? (*Customers were unhappy with how long it took a customer service representative to answer a call.*)

Solution: What did you do to solve the problem? (*I cross-trained more representatives.*)

Success: What were the results? (*Customer satisfaction improved by 60 percent.*)

APPLYING FOR A PROMOTION

The most important part of asking for a promotion is to be prepared to prove you are ready for the next step. Be able to articulate what you bring to the table. Make a list of all of your accomplishments to use as your talking points. You can't simply say you've done a great job in your current position; you have to show how you will do well in the next job. Most people are interested in what you will do for them.

One year after I made full colonel, I put in for a brigade command. My immediate superior was surprised. He said I should wait until I had more experience. I know he meant well, but I wasn't going to pass up an opportunity. I remembered Colonel Bacci's advice and knew I would lose nothing by applying.

I chose the Sixth Brigade as the unit I wanted to lead. I had heard that it was broken because of an unscrupulous civilian employee who was still in the unit. I knew that many officers did not want to take over a broken unit, so I put in for it. When you start at the bottom, there's no way to go but up. The command selection board agreed and selected me as brigade commander. It turns out I was ready for it, but if I had waited until I *felt* ready, the opportunity might have disappeared.

Sometimes it is difficult to determine who the decision maker is for promotions. I found useful a technique I had learned as a military intelligence officer. The Army had taught me to examine the Soviet military leadership structure to figure out who was in charge on paper *and* who was in charge in reality. We examined who had power and who had persuasion with the high command. We mapped the organization that existed on paper, and we mapped the shadow organization—the informal, unofficial organization of power. Analysis helped us discover who really had the ear of the commander. This technique can be useful in job promotions.

Look at the organizational chart. Examine who the players are. Find out who has the final approval for promotions. It usually rests with several people. Identify who has influence with those individuals. Gain insight into whom the boss listens to and respects. Locate those who can help advance your mission, your career, and your success. Do they know you in person or by reputation?

Once you have mapped the players, you need to cultivate relationships with the power players as an investment in your future. Figure out how you are going to meet and impress the power brokers. Get connected. Find out what each person's passion is. See if you can join in. It may mean taking golf lessons.

Get to know their schedule. Adjust your work schedule so that you run into the power brokers and are able to network informally with them. A friend of mine, Patricia, was one of many attorneys in a large organization. She watched, listened, and learned who had the power to help attorneys excel. She would take a different train home from the office so she could have informal conversations with key players. Constance cultivated her professional relationships and eventually moved from the general pool of attorneys to deputy chief counsel. When she became a partner, she was recognized for having her finger on the pulse of the organization.

Find opportunities for interacting. Offer to help on or join projects that are important to the decision makers. Coordinate with a peer who works for the power player to set up a coffee or lunch date with the three of you. Do not be shy about speaking to people at conferences or at training programs.

Find common ground. Relationship building begins with finding common ground or shared interests or experiences. Travel, family, pets, sports, and movies are topics to get started.

Pay it forward. I have learned that if I reach out to help someone, often he or she will return the favor in the future. As Stephen Covey explained in *The Seven Habits of Highly Effective People*, you need to build up the emotional bank account before you seek help from others. Invest in others before you ask them to invest in you. As a leader, you are much more than your job description. This is the time to show it. Show that you know how to cooperate, share important information, and lighten the load. If nothing comes back, it is OK. I believe that what you send out will come back eventually. If you help someone, someone (else) will help you. However, do not pay it forward for payback. Pay it forward because it is the right thing to do.

Leverage your political savvy. After you have built relationships and coalitions, you now have a network that can help you. Do not be afraid to ask for help. People like to help good people.

As a bonus, you can understand better the intricate system of power in your organization, rise above conflicts, build a reputation as a leader, gain access to resources, information, and opportunities, and influence outcomes. It is true organizational awareness.

BE STRATEGIC

Have the courage to ask early for the promotion. Be ready to talk about yourself with the Four S's: self, situation, solution, and success. Get to know the power players. You have to shine the spotlight on yourself; otherwise, you are sitting in the dark.

APPLYING IN WRITING

Sometimes, you'll need to write a formal cover letter to apply for a promotion. Aside from the content of the letter, make sure that the style, formatting, and editing are perfect. Texts and e-mails have helped to dumb down our writing, but understand that it really does still count to many people if you misspell words, don't know how to use a semicolon or comma, leave out the date on a formal letter, use lazy abbreviations, and so on.

Have your letter double-checked by a professional editor if possible, and if not, then seek out the nearest English teacher or librarian for proofreading and suggestions. Your résumé should also be up to date and carefully proofread for content, grammar, spelling, and formatting.

Stand out from the rest. Make sure your boss is aware of your accomplishments. Always be on task and complete assignments or projects on time and, if possible, under budget. Demonstrate leadership by volunteering for assignments. Be a team player.

Choose the right time. Don't throw it at the boss when there are projects overdue or he or she is getting ready to leave for a vacation. Make an appointment to discuss your performance and goals.

Be persistent. It may slip the boss's mind. Follow up. I find a reminder sent with "Is there anything else I can provide?" can help.

If the answer is no, don't give up. Find out what you might have lacked for the job so that you know how to better train or prepare for next time. Thank everyone involved in the process, regardless of the outcome. Writing a thank-you note or card is an especially nice touch and can also set you apart. It's rarely done these days, especially when someone has turned you down for a position.

HOLD YOUR OWN

Whatever weaknesses you may have, correct them. Don't give anyone an excuse to overlook you or not to take you seriously. Even if you think everyone accepts that you come in to work five minutes late most days, that could be all the proof a higher-up needs to show that you're not all that invested in your career and thus not worthy of a promotion.

Know whom you're competing against and how they can "beat" you. Know that there are certain physical characteristics that make someone seem like a natural leader: height, a deep voice, good posture, well-dressed. You won't be able to change your biology, but be aware of the differences and do what you can to compensate.

After I became the first woman brigade commander for the 84th Division, the division had a change of command ceremony. Each brigade formed on the parade field with the commanders in front. Since I was the commander of Sixth Brigade, my unit was the sixth in formation. General Smith gave out the command, "84th Division, Attention!" The First Brigade commander ordered in his deep, resonating voice, "First Brigade, Attention!" Then the Second Brigade ordered in his deep voice, "Second Brigade, Attention!" and on down the line. Now it was my turn; I looked at the viewing stand, and I saw women soldiers physically tense. I knew they were worrying whether I could be heard and heard well. In a deep, powerful voice, I ordered, "Sixth Brigade, Attention!" The women in the viewing stand relaxed. I had held my own.

Even if you can't afford a wardrobe of designer outfits, you can probably afford one or two. Invest in a couple of great suits or outfits that you can wear on strategic days—like when you're asking for a promotion! Wear platforms or heels if your height is not to your advantage.

If you can't be better than everyone else in some regard (e.g., you're not the fastest or the most experienced), then you have to sell yourself based on your potential or how you're different. Showcase what distinguishes you and provide as much quantitative as well as qualitative evidence as you can.

13

How to Survive
Unreasonable People

I received a thrilling call from the Pentagon in 2004: "Uncle Sam needs you." Saddam Hussein had been captured and was finally going before a judge to answer for his crimes against humanity. My assignment was to run the media center at Camp Victory where Saddam's trial would be held.

The evening before Saddam's trial, my cell phone rang. It was a representative from the U.S. State Department. He informed me that I was to wear civilian clothes. I replied, "Do you understand that we are in a war zone?"

He said, "Yes. Madame Secretary of State Condoleezza Rice would like you to wear civilian clothes to downplay the role of the military."

"Oh. Hooah."

Camp Victory had only one courthouse, and by the time I had escorted in star journalists, such as Christiane Amanpour, and representatives from Al Jazeera, there was no room for me. So I was outside the overcrowded courthouse in a long blouse and long skirt with combat boots when the bus transporting Saddam Hussein pulled up. The doors opened and Hussein got off the bus wearing a suit. Shackles bound his wrists and ankles. As he walked through the courtroom doors, his eyes were on the ground and his whole body was shaking. I looked at him and thought, "I bet he thinks he's going to die today." After all, that was Saddam Hussein's process of justice when he was in charge. I had actually stood on a stage where the floor was still sticky with blood, where Saddam sometimes gave someone the death sentence and then executed him on the spot.

I could not imagine what it must have been like to work for the man—to know that if you didn't follow his murderous orders, you might be next. An Iraqi friend of mine in Des Plaines had been one of Saddam's architects for his many palaces. He fled the country with his family after colleagues started to disappear. Working in fear was destroying his health.

Inside the courthouse, as soon as Saddam realized the Iraqi High Tribunal that had been appointed to oversee his trial would be more deliberate, he started screaming at the judge, telling him what he would do to him and his family and everyone in the courtroom when he was back in rightful power. This went on for a while until finally, the judge threw Saddam Hussein out of the courtroom.

As guards escorted Hussein out, he saw me in the hallway. Even though I was wearing a long-sleeved blouse and long skirt, he looked at me as if I were a bimbo just waiting to serve him. I could tell he was mentally stripping me naked. My stomach turned. I felt dirty. But as I began to avert my eyes, I caught myself. The way you look at a person can be an act of power or a sign of submission. When you look down or away from an aggressor, you're saying, "I'm not a threat." I wasn't going to let Hussein have this small victory at my expense. "No way, dude," I thought.

I don't know how to speak Arabic, so I had to rely on nonverbal skills to get my point across. I'm not a tall person, and in an Army full of bulky males, I'd had to learn how to carry myself. So I stared right back at him and straightened my spine while planting my combat boots firmly into the dirt. I made sure to relax my shoulders to let him know I wasn't intimidated. My message to him was, "Not this woman, buster. And guess what? You're going back to solitary."

At first, he just stared back at me as if I were an alien. I don't know how many women had stood up to him in this way. Finally, he broke eye contact and snapped out a command in Arabic that caused the guards to burst out laughing as they walked him back to the bus.

"Wait!" I caught up to one of the guards as he was leaving. "What did he say?"

The guard looked at me and said, "'Kill her.'" It turns out Saddam Hussein used to execute people who dared to stare at him. Even now, in shackles, he thought he was in charge.

General Ricardo Sanchez, who was the U.S. commander of coalition ground forces in Iraq, said that when he looked into the eyes of Saddam Hussein, he saw pure evil. I remembered General Sanchez's words as I looked into Hussein's eyes, but I didn't see pure evil. All I saw was a dirty old man whose only remaining power was idle threats.

I have met bad people who lack human decency. War zones can bring out the worst (and best) in people living under siege and terror of attack. But I have also encountered evil in the workplace. Now, a true psychopath like Saddam is very rare in business, but corporate sociopaths are common enough. In fact, sociopathy is estimated to affect 1 in 25 people, so odds are good you've encountered someone—a boss, coworker, or client—who lacks empathy and will do just about anything to get what he or she wants. Normal reasoning won't sway these people. Sometimes all you can do is get out of their sights. However, not everyone has the luxury of quitting a job or turning down a key assignment.

GENERAL MISERABLE

General Sanchez is a personal hero of mine. In 2004, Iraq was 30 years behind the world in communications, education, and technology. The media showed protests about the lack of electricity. What wasn't shown on TV was that under General Sanchez's command, our soldiers, sailors, Marines, and airmen rebuilt power plants, constructed schools, and trained men and women for police and military service. While the media showed car bombings, we were bringing science, technology, and law to the Iraqis—especially law. The media showed kidnappings, yet we were working to deliver freedom of speech, freedom of the press, freedom of religion, and the right to vote to the people. It wasn't all made for television, but Sanchez's leadership rested on the courage to do the right thing.

Unfortunately, not all leaders are of Sanchez's caliber. Before I departed the United States for Iraq, I had gone to the Pentagon for a briefing about my assignment and was warned that I would be working with a very difficult general officer. Fortunately, the briefer added, the general was not in my chain of command. In other words, I had to work with him, but he did not write my officer efficiency report. However, because he was senior to me, I had to do what he asked.

The first day I met General "Miserable" was in his office for the morning briefing. In the Army, officers are taught to let the soldiers eat first. The highest-ranking officers eat last. General Miserable did just the opposite. He would have us stand along the wall in his office at parade rest while he ate breakfast. This was a red flag for the days to come.

Every day, several times a day, he lashed out at people. He was a screamer and took pleasure ripping into people. One time, he threw a heavy-duty stapler at a lieutenant, hitting him in the head. The lieutenant refused to report the incident because he said the general had promised to send him home in time to attend special advanced officer training. He didn't want to lose the opportunity. I couldn't convince him that by reporting, he would be protecting others.

Every day we were subjected to the general's tantrums and verbal abuse. One evening, he lost his temper because he didn't know an important fact. Saying to the team, "I'm pissed because I wasn't informed" would have been fine. Instead, he turned into a three-year-old, stamped his foot, and had a tantrum in front of us. Respect for him was undermined by his lack of control.

I did a story for a major news outlet explaining how Brigadier General Janis Karpinski, the general responsible for the torture incident at Abu Ghraib prison, did not answer directly to General Sanchez. She answered to another three-star general. The media needed to understand the chain of command so as not to blame people who were not involved. General Miserable called me into his office, told me how stupid and wrong I was to say that she worked for another general, and then called a colonel to come in to hear how stupid Morgenthaler was. The general told him what an idiot I was and what I had told the reporter.

The officer looked at him and said, "Sir, she got it right."

He started screaming, "Why didn't I know this?" He did not understand that no one wanted to deal with a screamer. If people could avoid speaking to him, they did; therefore, he was ignorant of the facts. His public tantrums were so bad that foreign officers whispered to me that their countries would never have made someone like him a general officer.

The general complained about me daily to my boss, the Marine general Joe Weber. One morning at the staff meeting, General Weber looked at me and asked, "Morgenthaler, am I going to hear about you again today from General Miserable?"

I sat up straight and said clearly, "Yes, sir! And if I knew what I was going to do wrong, I would tell you what it was, and we would get it over with now."

The room laughed. People's opinion of me increased because I kept my composure and humor.

I tried to guide General Miserable because he had no media training. One afternoon, he ordered me to give breaking news only to Fox News because other media outlets such as the *Washington Post* and the *New York Times* were not writing favorable stories. I explained, "Sir, we shouldn't play favorites because it will backfire. It's our job to share the news with every outlet."

He barked at me, "I gave you a direct order. Now do it."

I tried again to explain how detrimental it would be if we denied powerful media players equal access to the news. He yelled again. I said, "All right. Put it in writing and I will clear it with the Pentagon."

"I don't have to put anything in writing," he said.

"Then I can't do it," I said. I stood my ground, and he backed off.

After General Miserable returned stateside, the Inspector General investigated a complaint about his poor leadership. The conclusion: that his leadership style was "occasionally inconsistent" with the standards expected for senior government leaders. The interesting point is that of all the people the investigators interviewed, they did not interview me, a colonel who worked with him every day. The real loss to the Army was at least one brilliant junior officer who decided to quit the military because of the abominable treatment he endured. I could not convince him that General Miserable was a fluke.

SIGNS OF A BAD LEADER

Dealing with poor leadership is especially challenging. One of the telltale signs that someone is a bad boss is when he or she walks through the office and people duck out of sight. Other poor leadership character traits include:

A lack of integrity. It does not matter how charismatic someone is; if he rationalizes unethical behavior, he will lose trust and may bring down the organization.

A lack of investment in the job or the people. Too often, someone takes a job solely for the tangible benefits, like a good salary or impressive title. However, if she does not invest her time and passion to leading, the team will fall apart.

Absence of accountability. Real leaders accept responsibility for failures that occur on their watch.

Self-serving nature. If a leader does not understand "we" but only "me," followers will not trust him and may not follow him.

Promise breaking. If a leader does not follow through on her commitments or promises, she will be deemed untrustworthy and not worthy of leading.

If a supervisor is a poor performer or a bad boss, subordinates may ignore him or her, may protest to the top, or may vote with their feet.

BAD BOSS TYPES

Unfortunately, too many people have to deal with unreasonable bosses. OfficeTeam staffing service conducted phone interviews to figure out what makes someone a bad boss and what happens to bad bosses' employees. They found that in about 38 percent of cases, the employee quit because of an unreasonable boss. The researchers identified five common types of bad bosses:

- **The micromanager** has trouble delegating tasks. This boss looks over your shoulder to make sure you complete a project *exactly* as told.

- **The poor communicator** provides little or no direction. Your assignments often have to be completed at the last minute or redone because goals and deadlines weren't clearly explained.

- **The bully** wants to do things his or her way or no way at all. Bosses like this also tend to be gruff with others and easily frustrated.

- **The saboteur** undermines the efforts of others and rarely recognizes individuals for a job well done. This supervisor takes credit for employees' ideas but places blame on others when projects go awry.

- **The mixed bag** is always a surprise. This manager's moods are unpredictable: he or she may confide in you one day and give you the cold shoulder the next.

With a micromanager, you need to build up trust. Complete all tasks on time and keep the individual well informed. After you have established a record of accomplishment, point out that you are ready to work more independently.

If you work for a poor communicator, make sure that when you are assigned a project, you get as much information as you can. Tactfully point out the details you need to ensure you meet expectations. Check in regularly to ensure you are on track. When in doubt, seek elucidation. Don't be shy asking for clarification.

I've dedicated a whole chapter (Chapter 8) to how to deal with a bully.

A saboteur may be one of the worst types of bosses. Ensure that you record your accomplishments on a biweekly basis or more with the boss and, more important, with senior management. Put everything you do in writing.

When a boss has mood swings, limit communications during the down days. Don't take it personally. Stay calm.

WHEN BAD BOSSES HAPPEN TO GOOD TEAMS

If you work for a bad boss, chances are you're not alone. On Wednesday nights, a group of colonels and I would gather to smoke cigars and share "war stories." I'm not a cigar smoker, but my husband would send me Cohiba cigars to pass around. It gave me a safe place to share my General Miserable stories.

Terrible situations can become tolerable with humor. It is why police officers have a dark sense of humor. It is a survival technique. In Iraq, when bombs exploded in our compound, we would look at each other and say, "Boom."

The worst thing that can happen with a bad boss is loss of trust throughout the entire team. Serving in the military during peacetime and war, I understood the value of trust. Every day, we put our lives in the hands of others, we watched each other's back, and we swore to leave no one behind. When I was in Iraq, after the story about the torture at Abu Ghraib broke, terrorists announced a bounty for capturing American soldiers. The reward for a male soldier was $3,000, for a female soldier $5,000. I worked with a wonderful woman major from the California National Guard. After the intelligence on the bounties was made public, we were discussing how neither one of us wanted to be captured, put in an orange jumpsuit, tortured, and beheaded on video. She and I made a pact that if our convoy was attacked and capture looked inevitable, we would each save two bullets. We agreed to shoot the other and then ourselves. Fortunately, it never happened. On that day, as we made the promise, I realized that I trusted her with both my life and my death.

On my last day in Iraq, I sat in the dining room of the palace having breakfast. I was disheartened by the increase in violence. The experiment in exporting democracy was endangering Americans and Iraqis alike. As I slumped over my breakfast, an Iraqi man who sat across from me asked, "Why do you look so sad?"

I answered, "I'm leaving today, and I don't see any improvements since I arrived."

He said, "Look around. Look at the young Iraqi women in the dining room."

I looked around and spotted small groups of Iraqi women in colorful blouses and dresses chatting with each other. I looked back at him.

"Do you see a difference in them since last year?"

I scanned the room. He was right. When I first arrived, the women were covered up in head scarves and long shapeless dresses, and they were scared. I nodded.

He explained, "They feel safe again. They can choose to wear what they want, they can go back to the university, and they can work. You helped do that."

For my leadership in Iraq, I received the Bronze Star. I often felt I got it because I survived such a bad boss.

SURVIVING A BAD BOSS

I recently spoke in front of several hundred college students. I asked them to raise their hand if they had worked for an unreasonable boss. Eighty percent of the hands shot up. Unfortunately, in life, sooner or later, you will deal with a bad boss. He may be a bully, or she may be incompetent. You need survival skills.

Start off understanding that your boss may not know he is a poor leader. It may be the circumstances, the lack of skills, or ignorance of employees' needs.

- Talk to your boss. But never tell him he is bad. That is guaranteed to backfire. Tell him what you need: goals, direction, feedback, and support. Stay calm, remain polite, and focus on your needs. Bullying does not disappear with wishful thinking.

- Ask her how you can help her be successful. Listen and act.

- If you are asked to do something unethical, put it in writing.

- If the person physically hurts someone, you must report it.

- If you see no improvement, go to your boss's manager and ask for advice and assistance. Or go to human resources and get recommendations on how to deal with the problem. Be aware that these are dangerous moves because your boss may never forgive you. Understand that, and ensure you have done all that you can do before taking your issues up the line. HR or the supervisor may not inform you about measures taken; therefore, allow time to see if the behavior improves.

- Have an intervention. Bring other colleagues who have experienced the bad behavior together to approach the boss, the supervisor, or HR. It's more compelling when there is more than one person suffering.

- If nothing changes, devise your exit strategy. Don't let the behavior affect your psyche. Everyone deserves to be treated with respect.

Many leaders lead with their heads instead of with their hearts. Often, men and women are praised for being tough and results-driven. That does not preclude being empathetic and compassionate, which means concentrating on people instead of systems. It means leading with respect and leaving no one behind. It means "mission first, people always." You go from "I" to "we." Here are ways to ensure that you will never be called a bad boss:

1. Stay connected to your team. Take time to engage in conversation.

2. Ask your team members what they need to get the job done and then try your best to get it for them.

3. Care for the well-being of others. Be flexible when people or family members are ill.

4. Share how you feel. When Secretary of Defense Donald Rumsfeld came to Iraq to meet with the media about Abu Ghraib, I told my staff honestly that I was anxious about us doing everything right, and when I'm anxious, I don't have a sense of humor. Be willing to admit you are human.

5. Put people before policies and procedures.

6. When you make a promise, keep it.

7. When you have done something wrong, own up to it.

8. When your team makes a mistake, you take responsibility.

9. When you succeed, you share the credit, recognition, and awards.

10. When you say, "I'm sorry," you do not add "but . . ." Adding "but" to an apology negates it.

11. Help the team to do its best and to be successful.

12. Always be hopeful.

13. Put "we before me."

Losing trust, unlike gaining trust, can happen in a moment. Once trust is lost, it is hard and sometimes impossible to gain back. Some of the actions that will cause people to lose trust in you are lying, taking credit for others' work, gossiping about team members, behaving erratically, avoiding blame, not apologizing for bad behavior, and showing lack of interest in the team or the mission. Unfortunately, there are so-called leaders who do all of the above. If you manage managers, stay alert. You do not want to lose good people because of a bad egg.

To recover trust, you must acknowledge what you did wrong, apologize with humility, and rectify what you did, if possible. Action must accompany words. "I blew it" is a very good start. "Here's how I will make it better" is a great next statement.

Create an environment of trust.

1. Live up to your standards before expecting others to do so.

2. Acknowledge your weaknesses and ask for help.

3. Share both good and bad news. The truth will come out, so do not hide information. If you cannot share, explain why.

4. Be transparent on assignments, missions, goals, finances, and resources.

5. Be consistent. Prioritize missions for the team.

6. Provide opportunities.

7. If in doubt, give the benefit of the doubt.

8. Shield the team by taking the blame.

9. Talk openly about your feelings.

10. Make personal sacrifices for the good of the team.

Understand that being the boss does not mean bossing people around. It is about facilitating the complex relationships with subordinates, peers, superiors, and people inside and outside the organization. You are a negotiator, not a dictator. Authority comes from your people embracing your vision and the mission. It is your credibility that will get the work done, not your orders.

Make respect a top priority. As much as I disliked General Miserable, I remained respectful. If you show disrespect, you lose your authority and damage your reputation. Never forget to look and act like a leader.

14

CRISIS LEADERSHIP

After my return from Iraq, I received an assignment that required me to wear two hats, homeland security advisor and deputy chief of staff for public safety for the state of Illinois. I was responsible for dealing with catastrophes across the state, whether the events were natural disasters, acts of terror, nuclear accidents, or man-made emergencies. I learned a lot about crisis management and how to lead effectively when everyone around you is freaking out. My military experience, leadership experience, and master's degree from the Army War College came into play as I led thousands of employees in keeping Illinois safe.

On my first day on the job, I realized that I had nine agencies reporting directly to me; these agencies ranged from a very small parole board to the state's Emergency Management Agency, Terrorism Task Force, Office of the State Fire Marshal, National Guard, Veterans Administration, Public Health, Department of Corrections, and Illinois State Police. Some of the agencies were in direct support of homeland security and others were not. I knew good leadership and teamwork were essential to dealing with any catastrophe that might arise.

Because I was an unknown quantity to the state employees, I had to start strong and quickly prove I was the right person for the position. I had to build my reputation from nothing and earn their trust before I could ask them to follow me.

When I met each agency head who reported to me, I asked questions and listened very closely. I had a lot to learn. My list of questions included:

How did you come to be in your position?

Tell me about your experience.

What projects are going well?

What challenges does the agency face?

What are some of the things I can do to help you?

The last question was the most critical. It's important to let people know that you're on their side and that you're there to help, not just to tell them what to do. If I could fix something quickly for the department, I would be able to establish my street cred immediately. State Police pointed out that a number of promotions were sitting in a computer system in limbo. I had the authority to push the promotions forward. As soon as I returned to the office, I did.

I let the directors speak as much as they wanted, and I took notes. When they shared with me personal information about their families and hobbies, I made a note of that, too, so I could ask in the future about them.

I found that building rapport paid off. People quickly became comfortable letting me know when they faced issues. The director of the Office of the Fire Marshal was the first to come to me with a problem. He was responsible for training paramedics around the state. A deputy at Public Health wanted to take over the program and use $1.4 million of the Office of the Fire Marshal budget to hire a contractor to apply standards that were not necessarily relevant to the state. The Fire Marshal told me that spending that much money was not justified. I looked into the matter and found he was right. I quashed the program. Years later, the deputy for Public Health went to federal prison for abuse of funds.

I was reminded of the value of teamwork when I worked with the courageous war hero (and present congresswoman) Tammy Duckworth, then head of the Illinois Department of Veterans Affairs. To build camaraderie, I invited her to attend meetings with the other agencies that focused solely on emergency response. Two of Tammy's strengths were initiative and a desire to learn. She came to every meeting. When the influenza pandemic became a national concern, the agency directors for the Illinois Emergency Management Agency and Illinois Department of Public Health tried to determine the best places to stage immunization shots across the state. Tammy threw out the brilliant idea that veterans homes could be staging areas, along with hospitals and community colleges. We accepted the idea immediately. This would not have been implemented had I not invited someone from a seemingly unrelated department to sit in on a crisis meeting. The teamwork was already paying great benefits.

BE A WALK-ABOUT LEADER

I could have sat at my desk, made phone calls, and scheduled meetings in my office, but instead I took the time to go to each agency and some subordinate departments. When you meet someone on his or her terms instead of your own, it's a sign of respect. Consider how much more meaningful it is to have a friend show up in person to check in on you rather than just call.

When I worked with members of the Prison Review Board, something very new to me, I had them walk me through a typical day and explain the acronyms, terms, and legal issues. I told them to treat me like their 13-year-old niece or nephew: someone bright but with no background.

Instead of asking the leadership of the Illinois Air National Guard to come to me, I drove to Scott Air Force Base. It was advantageous to see an organization in its surroundings. I got a feel for the morale, pride, accomplishments, and needs. After the 126th Air Refueling Wing commander explained that the mission was to support the U.S. Air Force by refueling jets, the Air National Guard took me up in a KC-135R and let me refuel a B-1 bomber. I would have missed that exciting opportunity if I had stayed in my office at the Capitol. (By the way, anyone who has played with a joystick can refuel a jet.) I came to call this leadership style the Walk-About Leader.[1]

You know who else is a great Walk-About Leader? Pope Francis! In a short time, Pope Francis has made major strides in improving the way people see the Catholic Church because of the way he stays in touch with the people he serves. He has led by example, not putting himself above menial labor, answering his mail, and calling people in need. In fact, he's been known to sneak out at night to break bread with the homeless. It's precisely because of how human and accepting he is that he is winning back people who turned away from Catholicism long ago. In a time of crisis when the church has dealt with numerous sex scandals and cover-

declaring zero tolerance for

RONYISM

ure you ca

nted people running each
use I trusted the people in

rk for success
k you lay with
g crises. This is
n within your

right person for the job.
I disliked the political
wledged that politicians
jobs for the Department
erior to leave the system
litician wanted me to hire

irector of the
ho was not a
was actively
gencies. He
and respon-
ways. They
nt over the

emergency operations in
d routinely to floods, tor-
en the position opened up,
ace.

b. A Coast Guard veteran who
neland Security applied. I inter-
rfect fit. I offered and he accepted
a politician from southern Illinois
t the job was his to fill, not mine. He
ernor screaming if I didn't back down.
He's my cousin's brother-in-law."

protection
promised
I kept my

stra
es.

y," he said. I called the candidate to tell him
e were related. He was confused but agreed.
t to play within the system—and to pick your
ght every wrong and fix every injustice. Pick the

ones that are most important to you and make s
with yourself for the rest.

WORKING TOGETHER FOR
THE GREATER GOOD

Good leadership and teamwork lay the groundw
during a time of crisis or change. The groundwor
your organization and people will pay off most durin
when mutual respect, trust, and open communicatic
organization are put to the test.

I had an open-door policy. One afternoon the d
Illinois Department of Natural Resources (IDNR), v
direct report, came to visit me. He had heard that I
learning about the security mission of different a
explained that his staff were law enforcement officers
sible for state parks and the security of Illinois wate
actively supported emergency response. He also we
resources IDNR had—boats, snowmobiles, and so on.

When I realized that IDNR was responsible for the
of waterways and was essential to homeland security,
to find emergency response dollars to help his mission
promise, which really paid off for the citizens of Illinois.

During an ice storm, hundreds of motorists were
at rest stops with no food, water, diapers for their babi
on. Calls were flooding the State Emergency Respons
We activated the state emergency operations plan. As we
long oval table working on rescuing the motorists, an II
son officer reminded us that IDNR had snowmobiles. W

A RED TEAM

As I ran homeland security, I studied the emergency response to Hurricane Katrina: what went well and what caused the loss of life and property. Several serious flaws existed among the various levels of leadership. Most important, the leadership was not willing to consider or prepare for the worst-case scenario: the breaking of the levees. The lack of worst-case scenario training was a sign that no one felt comfortable challenging authority.

Leading during a crisis requires rational, reasonable, and empathetic problem solving. Lieutenant General Russel Honoré, who in my opinion was the hero of Hurricane Katrina, reminds us in his book *Leadership in the New Normal*, "We have an innovative culture, an environment that supports critical thinking and inventing."[2] Cultivating critical thinking is an especially valuable tool during a crisis.

To push critical thinking, I turned to Andrew Velasquez, then the head of the Illinois Emergency Management Agency, and told him that I wanted him to be my Red Team—in other words, the devil's advocate. I had learned from the Army in Iraq that a Red Team has the mission to "continuously challenge plans, operations, concepts, organizations, and capabilities in the context of the operational environment and from our partners' and adversaries' perspectives."[3] I wanted to ensure that Illinois emergency response did not indulge in confirmation bias, the tendency to remember information in a way that confirms one's preconceptions.

Whom can you trust to be on your Red Team?

together with the American Red Cross and two state departments to get lunches, diapers, and medical kits flown to where the snowmobiles were staged. The snowmobiles then reached the rest stops and assisted the stranded. Understanding each other's strengths led to creative problem solving, but it wouldn't have happened if we hadn't laid the foundation months earlier.

PREPARING FOR HIGH EMOTION

Crises can cause people to react emotionally. During a tornado strike and simultaneous heat wave that affected southern Illinois, people and resources were stretched to the maximum. One evening, a young government official started yelling out of frustration. Maureen Cunningham, who was a legal advisor and the liaison for the Office of the State Fire Marshal, was in the command room during the outburst. She walked up to him and gently said, "Lead with the solution, not the emotion." He caught his breath, held it, and calmed down. "Lead with the solution, not the emotion" became a lesson that I have taken to heart.

When someone is overly emotional, make him or her stick to the facts. Challenge absolutes like "always" and "never." Resist the urge to escalate the emotion by yelling back or expressing shock. Model the right behavior by staying calm and getting to the crux of the problem—ask "reporter questions" (who, what, where, when, why) and attempt to talk through at least one possible solution rather than getting stuck discussing the minutiae of the problem.

Be careful that micromanagement does not come to the forefront during a catastrophe. A liaison officer from a support agency was dictating over the phone what supplies were needed, who had them, and how to get them. He started to tell the person on the other end of the line the step-by-step instructions on how to fill out the requisition form. I went up to him and signaled him to hang up the telephone. He looked surprised. I pointed to the list of other requirements that he hadn't gotten to yet.

"Why are you wasting time instead of simply delegating the task?" I asked. He admitted that he was micromanaging and acknowledged that the person on the other end was very capable.

During times of crisis, the temptation for a leader is to be a micromanager, but I have learned from my missions in combat zones that this is when you need to trust and to let everyone do his or her job. Micromanaging slows down the process and can cripple operations. Instead, rely on the experience of your team. People rise to the occasion. Remember, if you are the leader, the chances are good that it's because you have demonstrated appropriate judgment and decision making. Let others execute your decisions. You do not want delay between the decision and the action.

Also, micromanagement escalates everything to a crisis. Employees have a hard time determining when an event is really an emergency. By hiring the right people, training them, and empowering them, you can achieve fast and effective results without breathing down anyone's neck. Give them the freedom to solve problems on the spot, as well as the freedom to make mistakes as long as they learn from them. Freedom fosters creative problem solving, entrepreneurial endeavors, business acumen, and employee loyalty.

You can be helpful by asking what resources they need to complete the mission. People may not know at the moment what they need from you. Let them know it's okay to come back to you in the future when they have it figured out.

FOCUS ON RESULTS,
NOT METHODS OF GETTING THERE

One way to show that you're not going to be a micromanager is to convey that you trust your team. When a problem comes up, sit down with your direct report and agree to the results that are expected. Do not dictate how to do the job; just be clear on the end results. This gives him the ability to do it his way while providing the finished product. Coach instead of command.

Be consistent. Be clear on what you want, when you want it, and the quality required. I asked an engineer recently why he left what looked like a good job—excellent benefits, good retirement program, stock sharing, five weeks of vacation. He explained that his boss was inconsistent. On Monday, his boss told him to do something that would take two weeks full-time to complete. On Tuesday, he was told to do something else that would take days to complete. On Wednesday, he was told to drop everything for a different project. By Thursday, the boss was back to the Monday project. The yo-yo project management style was giving the engineer ulcers. Nothing was being done. Projects were over budget and over time. The only thing consistent was that the manager played the blame game, directing it at the engineer. As a result, the company lost a talented individual.

Make sure that your team members understand what you expect of them, both in regular times and in times of crisis. Will there be times they'll be asked to drop everything and work overtime? If so, what is their family support plan? Do you expect them to be available to communicate outside work hours? Be clear and consistent with your expectations, and take into careful consideration any objections. Try your best to work with your team to make sure that your expectations are reasonable and achievable.

QUASHING GOSSIP AND NEGATIVITY

Crises can bring out the worst in a team. You may find divides where there were none before—people who respond badly to pressure and take it out on other people, whether that's by lashing out verbally, gossiping, or being a negative drain on others.

Stop destructive behavior in its tracks and do not accept poor performance. Assertively point out what is wrong, and if possible, put it in writing. Provide positive feedback when the behavior ceases. Use respectful language and make clear what your expectations are. Remember, body language of nodding or staying silent will appear to mean you accept bad behavior. Don't allow someone to bring the rest of the team down with a torrent of complaints or negativity. You can't overlook it, or it can spread and ruin morale.

Some people are natural "catastrophizers," making a crisis worse by predicting that it's the end of the world. Redirect them quickly by saying, "We're not going to focus our energy on those thoughts. Our job is to fix this problem, and that's what we're going to do. Are you with me?"

On the flip side, if you have to deliver bad news, have the courage to do it in person. We've all heard stories of half a department being laid off via e-mail, which is one step up from announcing you want a divorce by text message.

Almost all companies will go through some level of crises, but handling a crisis well can mean you come out stronger on the other side.

15

REINVENTION

I have had to reinvent myself several times in my life. The first time was when I left active duty in 1981 and entered the U.S. Army Reserve and the civilian world. Three things had happened in West Berlin that convinced me that it was time to leave active duty. As my tenure as commander was coming to an end, I learned that one of the commanding generals was looking for a general's aide-de-camp. I knew that being a successful general's aide would give me exposure with high-ranking officers, would expose me to strategic planning, and could advance my career, so I went to the office to apply for the position. The present aide told me that only graduates of West Point could apply. I explained that I had joined the Army only as West Point was beginning to accept women, so I couldn't be a graduate of West Point. He said, "So what?" I was surprised that a general was unwilling to consider officers who had received their commissions elsewhere.

The second incident occurred because of another woman, stationed elsewhere, who had no connection to me. She proved that if one woman did something wrong, all women were tainted in the eyes of the Army. I had heard that an electronic warfare command on the Czechoslovakian border was available, and I had yet to do electronic warfare in my five years in the military. I wanted that experience.

I called my boss and told him that I wanted to extend my tour and take over the command. He stunned me when he said he would not recommend me. I asked, "Why not?"

He explained that the present commander was a woman who had just been relieved of command for alcoholism and sleeping with the first sergeant. I told him that he didn't have to worry about either one of those with me. I was not an alcoholic and my boyfriend was an officer. He said no—"I'm not making that mistake again."

I couldn't believe it. I was too shocked to ask him if the commander had been a man who was an alcoholic and sleeping around, would he hold that against all men?

The third incident occurred when I called the military intelligence branch officer to request a transfer to the Defense Language School with the goal of immersing myself in a language and getting my master's degree. I wanted to be a foreign affairs officer, fluent in either Russian or Chinese. I had aced the Defense Language Aptitude Battery, so I was eligible to learn either language. The branch officer said no. He was sending me to Texas to continue in COMSEC (communications security) because there were too few qualified COMSEC officers. I couldn't face the boredom of doing the same job for the sixth year in a row. It was time to reinvent myself.

In May 1981, I out-processed through Fort Dix, New Jersey. As I was sworn off active duty, I was sworn in as a Reserve officer. I headed to a Chinese language immersion program and graduated school on my own dime. The Monterey Institute of International Studies gave me a great education and helped me transition into the civilian world. I came into school a hard-charging alpha, trying to lead other students. I discovered that wasn't a successful style for meeting, studying with, and working with fellow students from around the world. People were scared of a military officer.

I learned to relax, smile more, and embrace the academic world. I admit I experienced a mixture of feelings about entering civilian life: fear, insecurity, anxiety, frustration, and loss. I wasn't accorded the respect I had enjoyed as a captain in uniform. I had to stop speaking in military jargon. I found that men were uncomfortable when I called them "sir" and women did not like being called "ma'am." I relearned to call people by their first names.

My second reinvention was not entirely by choice. In 2007, I led homeland security for the governor of Illinois, and federal indictments were piling up against him. This was not something or someone I wanted to be associated with, and I knew it was time to find a new job. I had worked too hard for too long to earn my good reputation.

Over the years, I had been approached to run for U.S. Congress. Congress needed proven leaders, people who could work both sides of the aisle, and veterans who put country and people before politics. From the sidelines, I watched an Illinoisan junior congressional representative vote against veterans, women, children, minorities, and gays. He voted to censor what our military members could watch and read. He voted against in vitro fertilization by specifying that a woman could carry eggs only one at a time, whether she conceived or not. He put corporations before people. I knew I could not let him go uncontested in the next election.

Running for Congress was the best of times and the worst of times. Looking back, I was Don Quixote tilting at windmills. My opponent was the incumbent, had $2 million in his reelection coffers, and was comfortable lying about me—which I did expect. His campaign literature claimed I was guilty by association with a corrupt governor. He also linked me to a man who had been indicted in 2006 for fraud, money laundering, and embezzlement. Although I had proved that I had never even met the man, he continued his lies. I had my symbolic Kevlar on, but unfortunately, my children took the lies personally. My son was so angry, I told him to quit watching television until after the election.

Like Don Quixote, I lost. The hardest part about losing was seeing the young people who had excitedly supported me break out crying when the results came in. On the positive side, I grew. I had studied the issues carefully and decided where I stood on each one. I went into the living rooms of the wealthy, the middle class, and the poor alike. I witnessed firsthand the struggles parents experienced raising children and caring for their parents at the same time. I observed the challenges teachers, small businesses, and small towns faced. I loved meeting the passionate young people who wanted to change the world.

VICTIM OR VICTOR

In 2008, I could not get a single job interview because I had worked for a governor who went to prison. I wanted to shake my fist at the sky. I wanted to lie down, curl into a ball, and give up. In my heart, I knew I would get through all this and come out a stronger person.

I just had to figure out what person I would become. Would I be a warrior or a wimp? A victim or a victor?

Being a victim would have been easy. I could stay in my pajamas all day, complain how life is unfair, and indulge in a pity party. Or I could choose to be a victor. I could get up every day and begin the job of re-creating who I was. I could live my mantra, "Times are tough. I am tougher." I was determined to be a hero who was temporarily down on her luck.

I developed a multipronged attack to getting work. I continued to apply for jobs, I began speaking to organizations about leadership, and I started my own emergency management consulting firm. The consulting work did not fulfill me. I missed the real world of saving and bettering lives.

I carefully examined what I was passionate about and what would fulfil me. In the 1990s, I had considered becoming a full-time professional speaker, but I was too afraid to leave a job and risk not having a regular paycheck. But now I had no job or regular paycheck to lose. Risk was attractive. I began speaking on leadership pro bono at Rotary Clubs, Chambers of Commerce, Elks Lodges, and other organizations. I ramped up my participation in Toastmasters International. I discovered that I liked researching and writing speeches as much as I enjoyed performing them. I created programs on leadership, leadership during crisis, and crisis communications. The paid gigs started coming in and kept coming in. When I walk onstage, I know I belong there.

When you find yourself at a crossroad, choose to be a victor, not a victim. The victim is the easy role. Instead of standing up for what is right, the victim rolls over. Instead of fighting for the people or the mission, she flees. Instead of taking action, he freezes.

MANTRAS FOR STRENGTH

It can really help to have a mantra that you repeat to yourself to set your intentions and keep your self-talk positive. My mantra is, "Times are tough. I am tougher." You might want to try one of these on for size:

"I can and I am."

"I am stronger every day."

"Trust the process."

"I am bigger than my fears."

"Today is my day."

"I was born for this."

"I am ready for greatness."

Victims are paralyzed by fear and powerlessness, and they often play the blame game: "It's her fault, not mine."

Many victims will use "If only . . ." as a mantra. "If only this had happened, I could have (fill in the blank)." A leader with a victim mentality will throw employees under the bus, will not stand up for what is right, and will whine instead of work toward a solution.

Being a victor is harder. Victors are heroes in life's journey. Heroes have the courage to put mission first and people always. They see a roadblock not as an obstacle but as an opportunity to push themselves to new limits and conquer what threatens to hold them back. A hero leads with the solution and not the emotion. He will stand up for himself without knocking others down. A hero will face an issue directly, exhibit curiosity about new ideas, and strive to keep an open mind. A hero stands up to the bully and reaches out a helping hand to the victim.

It is easy to be a hero when times are good, but tough when times are bad. Once you choose to be a victor, decide if you are meant to reinvent yourself. If you are facing an impossible blockade and you have tried many times and many ways to surmount it, maybe it's time to do something new. Instead of butting your head against the wall, step back and examine who you are, what you want to do, whom you want to be with, and what brings you joy. Reinvention is for any age.

1. **Imagine where you want to be.** If you don't know, that's OK. If you are young, be open and experiment. Now is the time for discovery. If you have been around the block, take the time to reflect on your experiences. Think about what you love to do and what you are good at, and see if you can find the perfect confluence between the two. A man I met was good at sales, spoke fluent Spanish, and loved the outdoors. He turned that into a job selling boats in the Hispanic and English-speaking markets.

2. **Once you know what you want, break the tasks into doable pieces.** When I decided to take the risk of being a professional speaker, I knew I had to improve my speaking skills and learn the business. I attended events. I took free classes, online classes, and training programs to enhance my skills. I reached out to those I wanted to emulate. I carefully chose organizations that could help me.

3. **Do the work.** I realized that I not only wanted to help people by speaking but also wanted to help those I could

not reach by writing a book about leadership. I started by blogging on leadership. I researched self-publishing versus traditional publishing. I wanted the book to be read around the world, and I knew that I would have a hard time making that happen if I self-published it. Following what successful, traditionally published authors advised me to do, I started by outlining the book and researching the literary agents specializing in leadership books. I prioritized which agents I wanted. I selected Lynn Johnston and wrote the query letter to her specifications. Although I mentally prepared to be rejected and start over, my first-pick agent agreed to represent me, and we put together a 60-page proposal. Casey Ebro at McGraw-Hill thrilled us when she accepted the book.

4. **Network.** Meet the people who are doing what you want to do. Reintroduce yourself to your social network to see what they are doing. It may spark an idea or open a door.

5. **Find a mentor who has done what you want to do.** He or she can share the reality of what steps you need to take and can give you perspective on what you seek.

6. **Emulate, do not imitate.** I have watched many fantastic speakers. I picked up tips and techniques and soon developed my own style of storytelling. Find your unique you.

7. **Volunteer.** Take a leadership position to help others and expand your horizons. Show up with your sleeves rolled up and learn something new. Become a problem solver. Pay it forward and pay it back.

8. **Tell the universe.** Let people know what you have in mind. My goals include speaking around the world. I have actively let people from India, China, the Middle East, Japan, and Vietnam know that I want to speak in their countries. We will see what happens.

9. **Have fun on the journey.** I took an hour-long improv workshop and saw the immediate benefits to enhancing my speaking, so I signed up for an eight-week course. It was fantastic. Every Monday night I was a kid again, while advancing my talents.

10. **Venture out.** Try new things, keep learning, continue discovering yourself, and always move forward.

Major life changes are never easy. Set new goals. Take real action. Embrace the journey. You'll like the new you.

Conclusion

As you move forward as a leader, you will face setbacks. Some may be due to no fault of your own. After 20 years of leading, I found myself back at ground zero—having to fight to do my job. It occurred in 1996, when I was in Bosnia. During that time, Sergeant Major Gene McKinney, the highest-ranking NCO in the Army, was stripped of his position because he had sexually abused lower-rank women. Major General David Hale was demoted two ranks for improper relationships with three wives of subordinate officers. Brigadier General Larry Smith had tried to grope Major General Claudia Kennedy, and his career ended when the allegations were proved true. Many male officers watched these men crash and burn. They started to treat military women with suspicion. We were possible Jezebels who would seduce them, make it public, and then destroy their careers. They saw the victims as the predators.

In Sarajevo, I learned that a two-star general would be the senior rater of my annual efficiency report. I went to the headquarters to introduce myself. He stepped out of his office and explained that he could not meet with me without a witness. He was not going to make himself vulnerable to false accusations. I was astounded and hurt. I had served honorably for 20 years; I had commanded units successfully; I had demonstrated courage under fire. Now, I was suspect? I knew I could not lead effectively if he did not trust me. I stood tall, took a deep breath, and said, "Sir, I have served honorably for 20 years. If you can't trust me, then send me home." He looked surprised. I added, "If, on the other hand, my 20 years mean anything, then let's compromise. When I meet with you, just leave the door open." The general thought about it, nodded, and said, "Hooah."

Just when you think you are done proving yourself, someone or something may get in your way. Courage is a daily requirement. Reapply leadership skills that have worked for you. Try new leadership strategies. Confront and conquer the obstacles in your way.

In this book, I have focused on three central themes: First, obstacles will block your path to success. You may choose to go over, under, or around them, but face them you must. It is the way you handle obstacles that will hone your skills, build your character, and prove your worth to the world.

Second, if you wish to lead, you must gather the inner courage to speak up and stand up for yourself. Never did I accept the limitations that others tried to impose on me, whether in the military or in my civilian work.

Leadership in four words:
Mission First, People Always

Leadership in three words:
Compassion, Confidence, Competence

Leadership in two words:
Hope, How

Leadership in one word:
Respect

Third, as a leader, it is your responsibility to watch the backs of those you lead. Leave no one behind. Speak up for those who are not in power. Leadership is respect for those who follow you.

Notes

Chapter 2

1. National Education Association, "Research Spotlight on Single-Gender Education," www.nea.org/tools/17061.htm.

Chapter 3

1. Jack Zenger, "We Wait Too Long to Train Our Leaders," HBR Blog Network, December 17, 2012, http://blogs.hbr.org/2012/12/why-do-we -wait-so-long-to-trai/.

Chapter 6

1. Associated Press, "Frozen with Fear? Science Tells Why," updated October 30, 2007, http://www.nbcnews.com/id/21547710/ns/health -mental_health/t/frozen-fear-science-tells-why/#.U8bnVfldWSo.
2. Scott O'Grady and Michael French, *Basher Five-Two: The True Story of F-16 Fighter Pilot Captain Scott O'Grady* (New York: Yearling, 1998).

Chapter 7

1. Amy J. C. Cuddy, Caroline A. Wilmuth, and Dana R. Carney, "The Benefit of Power Posing Before a High-Stakes Social Evaluation," Harvard Business School Working Paper, No. 13-027, September 2012, http://dash.harvard.edu/bitstream/handle/1/9547823/13-027.pdf? sequence=1.

Chapter 10

1. Randy Pullen, "Breaking Through to Lead the Way: Women in the Army Reserve," [army] *Digest*, March 6, 2000, https://groups.google .com/forum/#!topic/sci.military.moderated/nmreoeIdJ9E.

Chapter 11

1. See www.123magic.com/.

Chapter 14

1. "Walk-About Leader" and "Walk-About Leadership" copyrighted June 2014 by Jill Morgenthaler.
2. Russel L. Honoré with Jennifer Robison, *Leadership in the New Normal* (Acadian House Publishing, 2012), 117.
3. U.S. Army Training and Doctrine Command (TRADOC), www.tradoc .army.mil.

Index